The Law and
Vulnerable
Elderly People

CONTENTS

The Law and
Vulnerable
Elderly People

© 1986 Age Concern England
Bernard Sunley House
60 Pitcairn Road
Mitcham, Surrey CR4 3LL

ISBN 0 86242 050 4

First impression 1986
Second impression 1987
Third impression 1989

Designed by Eugenie Dodd

Printed by Grosvenor Press, Portsmouth

Preface

Some twelve to fifteen years ago, when my work was more closely connected with children at risk than with the older generation, much of the debate among professionals and informed lay people was concentrated on defining situations of risk and abuse amongst the young. They were trying to find ways of protecting the interests and ensuring the welfare of this group by introducing appropriate legislation, and through involving them, their caring relatives and others close to them in plans for their future. Even then there was a noticeable gap between the positive attitudes towards children those discussions reflected and the way older people were viewed.

Only now are we beginning to acknowledge that an approach, similar in some respects, but avoiding the danger of 'infantilizing' adults, is vital if we wish to be of real help to the growing numbers of very elderly people amongst us. That so many people survive into old age is a major achievement of the twentieth century, but a significant minority of them will become vulnerable. These are the people about whom this report is written. They are difficult to define precisely, but we have all come across them among our friends or within our families. Many of them seem to slip through the welfare net of available service provision.

In seeking to give them a stronger voice this report raises a number of questions and highlights certain dilemmas we all must face if we are to ensure to vulnerable old people a quality of life we would find acceptable ourselves. One day any one of us may be amongst those people forced to experience our success or failure in achieving this.

Not everyone who reads this report will agree with the suggestions it puts forward, but I hope it will stimulate interest and raise awareness about people who tend to be forgotten and are sometimes neglected as we concentrate on others with a higher profile.

It would be impossible to express my thanks adequately to all the people who have been involved in the lengthy process of consultation and work which this report has involved. All the members of our expert group, advisers and external consultants, have been more than generous with their time and in sharing their skills and expertise with us, providing thoughtful advice as well as offering constructive criticism. While it is difficult to single out individuals, there are a few whom I would like to mention specifically:

Hilary Kates has spent an enormous amount of time with me extending over weekends and long evenings, formulating ideas in detail. She compiled the first draft of the report and her support and help have been invaluable.

Simonetta Hornby's practical legal expertise was extremely important in refining the basic ideas which were the springboard for the whole exercise. Evelyn McEwen's help was essential in ensuring factual accuracy, and in helping to construct a logical structure for the book. Jill Manthorpe's extensive research and her collaboration with Hilary and myself in writing up the final report were greatly appreciated. I also want to acknowledge with gratitude the skill with which Christine Blane amassed information and deciphered comments from a whole group of people whose ideas, enthusiasm and recommendations were inevitably far better than their handwriting. Her work extended far beyond the word processing job she thought she had taken on.

Lastly, I want to thank David Hobman, Director of Age Concern England, whose encouragement, patience and support throughout made it all possible.

Sally Greengross

July 1986

Acknowledgements

CONSULTATIVE GROUP ON THE LAW AND THE RIGHTS OF VULNERABLE ELDERLY PEOPLE

MEMBERS OF THE GROUP:

Sally Greengross, (Chairman) Deputy Director, *Age Concern England*

William Bingley, Assistant Director – Legal Affairs, *National Association for Mental Health (MIND)*

Dr Richard Grimes, Solicitor, Lecturer, *University of Keele*

Simonetta Hornby, Solicitor

Dr Peter Jefferys, Psychiatrist, Mental Health Commissioner

Christopher Johns, Principal Officer, Services for Elderly People, *Wiltshire Social Services Department*

Hilary Kates, Barrister, *Carematch Residential Care Consortium*

Evelyn McEwen, Head of Information and Policy Department, *Age Concern England*

Alison Norman, Deputy Director, *Centre for Policy on Ageing*

Diana Peeler, *British Association of Social Workers*

Dr Mary Piper, Consultant Physician in Geriatric Medicine, *Harrow Health Authority*

Dr John Scriven, General Practitioner

EXTERNAL CONSULTANTS:

John Eekelaar, *Pembroke College, Oxford, Faculty of Law*

Professor Ian Kennedy, Professor of Law, *King's College, University of London*

Mrs A B Macfarlane, Master of the Court of Protection

Norman Marsh QC, *Vice-Chairman, Age Concern England, Former Law Commissioner*

Professor Olive Stevenson, *Vice-President, Age Concern England, Professor of Social Work Studies, University of Nottingham*

ADDITIONAL ADVICE GIVEN BY:

John Bettinson, Solicitor, *Member Age Concern England Executive Committee*

Mervyn Eastman, Divisional Manager (North) *London Borough of Enfield Social Services Department*

Leo Goodman, Director of Social Services, *London Borough of Wandsworth*

Ruth Lavery (née Trimble), Law Lecturer, *Queen's University, Belfast*

Professor Martin Lyon Levine, *The Law Center, University of Southern California, USA*

Professor Peter Millard, Professor of Geriatric Medicine, *St George's Hospital, London, Member Age Concern England Executive Committee*

Judith Oliver, The Association of Carers

Ivor Walker, Solicitor

Advice and help were also given by Age Concern Scotland, Age Concern Northern Ireland and Age Concern Wales

Research undertaken by: Jill Manthorpe

It is the needs we have created for ourselves,
and the language of entitlements
we have derived from them, which give us any claim
to respect and dignity as a species,
and as individuals.

MICHAEL IGNATIEFF
The Needs of Strangers

INTRODUCTION

A DEFINITION OF VULNERABILITY

'Elderly people in need of some support, help and/or advice in order to prevent or postpone "personal or social deterioration or breakdown". Without this their level of dependency on others or their ability to manage their lives as they wish might deteriorate to the point of necessitating their removal to institutional care, which is not their preferred option and might otherwise be prevented or postponed'.

See Section Five Chapter Two page 128.

Chapter One

The Law and Vulnerable Elderly People

1 INTRODUCTION

1.1 The ageing of the population represents one of the greatest challenges of modern society. In Britain, whilst the numbers of people of 60 to 74 will remain fairly static over the next 40 years, those of 75 and over will increase by more than one third. It is amongst people of 85 and over, however, that the most spectacular increase will take place. In the last 20 years of this century their numbers are expected to double to almost one million.

1.2 In the light of such dramatic demographic changes, we need to ask ourselves whether we have the legal framework within which a humanitarian set of social goals can be realized, or if the increasing numbers of very old people present a new situation which our legal and social mechanisms were not constructed to serve. Changing social circumstances may require changes in the procedures prescribed by the law. Current legislation (1986) which is directly related to elderly people is listed in Section Five, Chapter One.

1.3 It is recognized that no legislation can ensure good practice, as recent cases of child abuse clearly demonstrate. However, there are at present groups of elderly people, rendered vulnerable through progressive physical or mental frailty, or in a situation of potential exploitation by others through economic or emotional dependency, who have little legal protection. Those caring for them are similarly deprived when compared with carers of other dependent groups in the population. There are problems of balancing the need for care and protection of these vulnerable old people against the potential dangers of infantilizing them; such controversial and at times fundamental issues need careful consideration and this report will attempt to highlight them and promote further discussion.

1.4 In many countries,[1] these and related issues are now beginning to be widely debated. There is a growing awareness of the need to find effective mechanisms to deal with the changing population structure, in which many more handicapped and dependent people live into extreme old age. These are therefore matters with far-reaching ethical and moral implications. It is hoped that this report will interest groups of people who have not previously considered these issues in any great depth, and help to increase awareness of the difficulties faced by professional workers and practitioners as well as carers, formal and informal, working in the community. Their devotion to caring for vulnerable and frail people over a long period is not always backed up by an adequate legal framework. Elderly people and those who care for them should have the same rights to planned care and services as other groups of people in need.[2]

1.5 There are, of course, many excellent examples of constructive work to be found when thorough assessments are followed by balanced decisions and the planned care of vulnerable old people. It might therefore be suggested that 'good practice' would remove the necessity for any legal framework. However, good practice may be partly dependent on an adequate provision of services and support

---

[1] See, for example: Leonard D Cain, *'Human Rights and Older Citizens' Rights'*, Portland State University, Oregon, USA (Paper presented at the 11th International Conference of Gerontology, 1984)
Law and Old People in Australia: An Overview, Australian Council on the Ageing, 1983
The Role of the Elderly in the Family in the Context of the Society of the 1980s, Council of Europe, Conference of European Ministers Responsible for Family Affairs, September 1983

[2] See, for example, the arrangements for health care in the local authority homes studied by the Social Services Inspectorate of the Department of Health and Social Security, 1985, *Inspection of Local Authority Care for Elderly Mentally Disordered People*. Few residents had routine checks of hearing aids, few had speech therapy, visits from dentists, domiciliary physiotherapists, and the community psychiatric nursing service was described as 'patchy' (Section 6.2).

and vulnerable old people may fall victim to a level of 'discretion' determined more by resource allocation than by a response to their real needs. A legislative framework of procedures could at least ensure that they have an entitlement to a minimum level of care and support.

2 WHO ARE THESE VULNERABLE ELDERLY PEOPLE?

2.1 This is an age of uncertainty when some of the definitions to which we were accustomed are now becoming meaningless. It is increasingly difficult to know what is meant by 'old' or 'elderly'. In previous times such terms usually denoted those who had passed retirement age. Today, with improved medical care, rapid industrial change, increasing unemployment and redundancy, and more very old people, such clear definitions are difficult to draw. The time span of retirement extends for many people to 30 or 40 years. People who have retired at a relatively young age tend to be active and vigorous participants in, and members of, their community. We shall concentrate here on the vulnerability which is frequently associated with extreme old age and the dependency it brings. For a definition see page 128 para 1.1.

2.2 This report is concerned, therefore, with elderly people who are vulnerable. Elderly people can become dependent on others through physical disability, various functional mental disorders or depressive states, chronic sickness, poverty, or lack of access to the facilities and support services that they need. Dependency on others can make people vulnerable to abuse or neglect either in a family or in an institutional setting.

2.3 The following table[3] illustrates the way in which physical disability creates dependency and vulnerability as people age, in that many become increasingly unable to go out alone, to climb stairs or to deal with the basic tasks necessary to independent living.

---

[3] *General Household Survey* (1980). (Revised estimates of dependency and disability will be provided by the General Household Survey (1985.)

PERSONAL MOBILITY

Percentage usually unable to manage on their own by sex and age*
persons aged 65 and over   *Great Britain: 1980*

ACTIVITY		AGE					
		65–69	70–74	75–79	80–84	85 & OVER	ALL 65 & OVER
Going out of	Males	3	7	8	15	[20]	7
doors and walk-	Females	6	10	16	32	51	15
ing down the road	All elderly	5	8	13	26	48	12
Getting up and	Males	2	5	5	12	[17]	5
down stairs and	Females	4	6	11	18	31	9
steps	All elderly	3	6	9	16	31	8
Getting around	Males	1	2	1	2	[6]	1
the house (on the	Females	1	1	2	3	10	2
level)	All elderly	1	1	1	3	10	2
Getting to the	Males	1	2	1	2	[6]	2
toilet	Females	1	1	3	4	9	2
	All elderly	1	1	2	3	9	2
Getting in and	Males	1	2	2	4	[7]	2
out of bed	Females	1	1	2	2	9	2
	All elderly	1	2	2	3	10	2

* Brackets [ ] represent actual figures, not percentages.

3 THE CHALLENGE OF SENILE DEMENTIA

3.1   Dependency is highlighted in the case of old people suffering
from the various forms of dementia. It is hoped these will be
preventable in the not too distant future, but there is no cure
at present, although it may be possible to slow down the
process of deterioration. More than 22 per cent of people
over 80 suffer from some degree of dementia.[4] Typically it
progresses slowly and can take many years to develop fully,
although it may be more rapid if due to cerebrovascular disease.

[4] *The Rising Tide – Developing Services for Mental Illness in Old Age*, Health Advisory
Service, 1982; *Mental Illness in Old Age*, Alison Norman, Centre for Policy on Ageing,
1982.

3.2   In its early stages, sufferers may be forgetful and find it difficult to manage their own affairs and lives effectively without varying degrees of support. However, in familiar surroundings, and with appropriate help, many do continue to live at home, coping with everyday life over a long period. To label such people at this very early stage as 'mentally ill' is often, therefore, inappropriate. Because of their numbers and the frequency with which people will encounter this condition amongst their relatives and friends, perceptions and attitudes need to be reviewed.

3.3   Dementia has profound implications not only for those suffering from it, but also for their carers. As some degree of dementia is now the likely outcome for one in five people who live into very old age, this needs to be better recognized and appropriate mechanisms and safeguards to deal with its effects are essential.

3.4   It should be acknowledged that elderly people who are slowly becoming demented have needs which change as their illness progresses and their views should still be sought whenever possible. They may become increasingly vulnerable because of the dependent situation in which they live, open to abuse, exploitation or neglect by other people. They may also be vulnerable through inadequate health, social services or housing provision appropriate to their needs or through shortcomings in existing legal procedures.

3.5   There is little legislation that is directly relevant for use in such circumstances. Procedures under existing mental health legislation are often inappropriate in dealing with the early stages of this slowly progressive condition which cannot be cured.

3.6   People diagnosed as suffering from dementia are covered by the provisions of the Mental Health Act (1983). This gives a framework for the protection of patients' rights, while enabling carers and professional workers to provide treatment and care. The Act recognizes the duty of care which professionals owe to patients with mental illness. There is, however, a 'grey area' when, for example, old people cannot be described as 'demented' but rather as slightly confused or mentally frail. Others may be physically frail and/or dependent and may be vulnerable or even at risk. It is questionable whether it would be appropriate to treat such people under the Mental Health Acts, and without recourse to the extreme measures of Section 47 of the National Assistance Act (1948) there is no legislation designed to ensure that their needs are met. In the United States, the term 'semi-incapacitated' is being used in trying to identify these people in law as a defined group.

3.7   It is a misconception to think that all vulnerable elderly people suffering from physical or mental frailty can, should, or wish to be, looked after in hospital or in nursing or residential homes. Under four per cent of retired people live in long-term institutional care in this country; most will remain in the community, on their own or supported by relatives.[5] When they do need some form of long term institutional care, it is often very difficult to arrange for them to be admitted. Many remain living in the community, but in need of support, which they do not receive.[6]

4 HISTORICAL ROLE OF THE STATE

4.1   It is widely, and often incorrectly, assumed that in an idealized and somewhat mythical past, elderly people were always cared for by their families, but in fact until recently very few people survived into extreme old age to be in need of such care.[7] Life expectancy has increased dramatically and medical progress has made it possible to prolong the lives of many chronically sick and frail people. However the pre-requisites for ensuring that they enjoy an acceptable quality of life are not always readily available. Familes are often expected to continue giving largely unsupported care for as long as 15 or 20 years, frequently with no access to the help and support they need.

---

[5] *Caring for the Elderly and Handicapped: Community Care Policies and Women's Lives*, Equal Opportunities Commission, 1982

[6] See, for example, the report of the Royal College of Physicians by the College Committee on Geriatrics, 'Organic Mental Impairment in the Elderly', reprinted from the *Journal of the Royal College of Physicians of London*, Vol 15, No 3, July 1981

[7] Pat Thane, 'Old Age in Victorian Britain', in *New Age*, Summer 1985. Thane highlights the fact that in 1851, 4.6 per cent of the UK population was over 65.

4.2 Even in today's constrained economic climate a greater degree of social awareness exists, recognizing that individuals cannot always be expected, or be able, to cope on their own. As a result, over the years, the State, at a national or local level, has increasingly assumed wider responsibilities and duties. Nevertheless, most elderly people wish to continue living at home regardless of any limitations this may place on them. It is also now generally accepted that there are limits to the demands the community can impose on its individual members. However, the functions and responsibilities of the state are limited, not only by resources, but also by the competing desire of many people to look after their elderly relatives themselves, often in the face of tremendous problems.

4.3 If these problems become insuperable, vulnerable old people or their carers may feel unable to continue to cope. In such circumstances, how does a responsible society best fulfil its obligations to them? Protective intervention, if based solely on codes of 'good practice', might place vulnerable elderly people too much at the mercy of the institutions of the state however benevolent they may be.

4.4 A system is needed that would give vulnerable old people and their carers access to a network of support and help, if their needs are not being met. They have a right to the same level and quality of services and medical and social care as other age groups in the community. Legally enforceable rights, however minimal, could possibly be protected through representatives who could speak on behalf and defend the interests of those old people who become unable to do this for themselves.

4.5 There is sometimes a tension between the protection of the welfare and the representation of the interests of this vulnerable group of people in our society. Vulnerable old people are often dependent and in this respect have something in common with children as both groups may need protection and support through outside intervention. Any such intervention by another must inevitably reduce self determination, and can be seen as an infringement of individual liberty. In the case of children this is generally accepted but in the case of vulnerable elderly people, however necessary such protection may be, it is always essential to recognize and acknowledge their adult status. Every effort must always be made to obtain their consent to, and cooperation in, any action that is planned or taken.

4.6 There are already certain legal provisions imposing mandatory duties and responsiblities on individuals and statutory bodies for the care and welfare of children. In almost all cases the welfare of the child is paramount in determining any action to be taken.

4.7 Parents who for some reason are unable to cope with a child can turn to someone for help, whether this involves a statutory or voluntary body or the legal system.[8] They can if necessary place the child voluntarily in the care of the local authority, which is obliged to accept that responsibility if it is necessary in the interests of the welfare of the child.[9]

4.8 Whilst normal children will outgrow their minority status and thereby achieve adult rights, a frail old person is likely to become progressively more dependent. It is, therefore, vitally important to safeguard and, if necessary, *enhance* that person's rights.

4.9 Relatives or carers also need a mechanism giving *them* access to help if they can no longer cope. They need to be assured that, in such an event, appropriate services will be alerted and help and advice brought to their assistance. There are at present very few statutory duties laid on local authorities in relation to vulnerable adults.

4.10 The existing provision is generally permissive rather than mandatory and present procedures, once set in motion, tend to protect people considered to be at risk in some way, at the expense of their rights as adults to self determination. Existing statutes are frequently inadequate in law in the

---

[8] Though many would not agree with the assertion that children are protected adequately, see, *The Rights of Children*, ed B Franklin, Basil Blackwell, 1986

[9] Section 2(1)(b) Child Care Act (1980) provides for voluntary reception into care, and under Section 3 of the Children and Young Persons Act (1963) a parent may apply to the court for an order directing the local authority to institute proceedings under Section 1 of the Children and Young Persons Act (1969) when the local authority had previously refused to do so.

situations where they are used and the line between the loss of independence and protection against ill treatment or abuse is a difficult one to draw.

4.11 The drastic action invoked by the use of Section 47 of the National Assistance Act (1948), which allows compulsory removal from home in extreme circumstances, makes many local authorities unwilling to use it, resulting in only approximately 200 cases a year. It is an extreme example of protection without representation and in many cases it may seem to be 'protecting' professional workers, neighbours and others at the expense of the right to self determination of the elderly person concerned. The result of such intervention can have far-reaching effects, disproportionate to the risk resulting from, for example, living in insanitary conditions. Once people are removed from home and relocated they may have no further opportunity to make fundamental decisions about how or where they wish to live and become rapidly institutionalized.

4.12 The Court of Protection (See Section Three, Chapter One) is still frequently a mystery even to otherwise well informed professionals, although efforts are being made to broaden and publicize its activities. The ancient origins of the Court have left us with the legacy of an institution primarily concerned with the affairs of people with more than a specified amount of money. The Court does not have the resources necessary to enable it to monitor or respond to the immediate needs of its 'patients'.

4.13 Guardianship (See Section Three, Chapter Two) under the Mental Health Act (1983) confers on the guardian, largely through local authorities, the right to make certain decisions for someone who is adjudged to be suffering from serious mental disorder. In appropriate cases guardianship can provide a mechanism both to protect the interests of people and place them under some control.

4.14 These procedures all allow intervention into the immediate life of an elderly person who is seen to be at risk. They all entail decisions being taken by someone else – decisions which may be made despite the wishes of the person about whom they are taken.

4.15 In contrast to those legal procedures which permit action by statutory authorities, there are others through which an elderly person can choose someone to participate in decision-making or simply pass on rights in a limited way to facilitate particular actions.

4.16 One example of limited representation is that of Agency (See Section Four, Chapter One) which thousands of people use to allow someone else to collect money when, for some reason, they are unable to do this for themselves: a frequently used example is the collection of pensions for disabled elderly people. These agents could perhaps be enabled to extend their role, if required, to include, for example, some form of limited advocacy.

4.17 Appointees (See Section Four, Chapter Two) have defined rights to act for people who are unable to manage their own affairs, but these are limited to collecting and dealing with payments under the Social Security Act (1975), Section 81 and the Supplementary Benefits Act (1975), Section 14. The appointee acts on behalf of, and for, the person concerned in these circumstances, and provides an administrative convenience, particularly for residential homes and hospitals, but there is no formal monitoring of the system. Elderly people who have appointees are dependent upon their honesty and reliability, but it is a relatively simple procedure, useful in appropriate situations.

4.18 A Power of Attorney (See Section Four, Chapter Three) confers certain legal rights on another person, the donee, allowing that person to act for the donor. This may be limited to a specified transaction or be granted as a general Power. It is only valid in law while the person giving it is fully mentally competent. If the donor subsequently becomes mentally incapacitated, the Power is no longer valid but in practice many donees unknowingly continue to act for the donor in such circumstances. People giving a Power can undoubtedly be represented as they would wish, as they specify the terms and conditions of the Power, but they lack protection if the Power is used after it should have been automatically revoked following their mental incapacitation. By contrast the new Enduring Power of Attorney continues to be valid after supervening mental incapacity but only if it was created before the donor lost mental capacity. Therefore it can only safeguard those who plan ahead and can find a nominee.

4.19 There are two existing 'representatives' within the legal system who may be called upon in certain circumstances. The official solicitor can act for people in litigation if they are incapable of giving instructions and is often requested by the Court of Protection and other courts to represent an incapable person in hearings at that Court. He has a duty to consider a case but need not take it on. At present his office is busy, working on a tight budget with a small staff. There is also concern about who should meet his costs.

4.20 Court welfare officers represent the interests of some mentally ill people in court, particularly when other parties are already represented by the official solicitor. They are usually social workers or probation officers who prepare reports. The court can ask a welfare officer to help provide evidence of a person's wishes. The welfare officer may appoint a solicitor to act if that person needs legal representation. Court welfare officers deal mainly with children. They have no specific training, nor opportunity to acquire the necessary skills to work with confused elderly people. To protect such people adequately a representative would need to develop a personal knowledge of their needs and desires, through personal contact over a period of time, to be able to determine, and thus represent, their best interests.

4.21 An example of representation provided by the voluntary sector is the scheme set up by the Advocacy Alliance (see Addresses on page 140), which enables someone to act in the interests of an individual patient in an institution. This service was established as a result of increasing recognition of the need for support for the many thousands of mentally handicapped people living in long-stay hospitals, who receive no support from the community. A few small experimental schemes have been set up, and these might serve as one model for the representation of elderly mentally frail people. Under another model, a panel could represent the interests of a group of patients or long-stay residents. It might even act for all patients or residents in a hospital or residential home.

4.22 On the other hand, as most elderly people remain at home, their interests also need to be protected, possibly through some specialized system of representatives.

4.23 These representatives could be one or a combination of the following, depending on the particular circumstances and their experience and/or qualifications:

1 individual advocates (legal or informal);
2 specially trained and recognized social workers, medical practitioners or other suitably qualified people;
3 volunteers, administered through the legal system, social services or voluntary organisations;
4 members of the family, or friends.

4.24 Before such representation could take place the following would need careful consideration:

1 that there is a recognized need for such representation;
2 that there are adequate procedures for its institution;
3 that there are safeguards to protect the interests of the elderly people in question.

4.25 The recurring theme in this report is the relationship, and in many cases the tension between protection and representation. At present, under most existing legislation, there is *no requirement* for consultation between all interested parties, nor are there adequate incentives to bring in the necessary support services as a prerequisite to taking drastic action, which often proves to be irreversible.

4.26 The need to protect vulnerable elderly people, although very important, cannot justify the denial of their right to be consulted, either directly or through someone who is in the best possible position to ascertain their wishes. Otherwise protective action may be more for the benefit of people acting 'in the best interests' of others, than for vulnerable elderly people themselves, who are thereby denied the adult status to which they are entitled.

4.27 Underlying much of this discussion is the fundamental question of consent. In some circumstances the law allows action to be taken which dispenses with the right of the person concerned to refuse that action. Mentally or even physically frail elderly people may be considered incapable of making informed decisions, but they have the right to decide for themselves whenever possible. If decisions which affect their lives are to be taken by someone else, every effort must be made to ascertain their wishes even if ultimately it is considered justifiable to override them for some reason.

4.28 Competent adults who are not under duress are assumed, in what they do, to be acting voluntarily, and, in what they allow to be done to them, to be giving their consent. In contrast, someone who is vulnerable, whether through age or through physical or mental infirmity, may find that action is taken without such consent being sought. Vulnerability can increase the likelihood of things being done *to*, rather than *by*, a person. It may make a person a potential victim, whether of circumstances or action. Thus, an accumulation of circumstances for such people may distort the view of what constitutes valid consent. Vulnerable elderly people are, by reason of their age or infirmity, more likely to face decisions directly acknowledging their own frailty.

4.29 Consent may only be meaningful if there is an element of choice between the options presented. A decision to go into residential care (See Section Two, Chapter Three) is intrinsically tied to the recognition of personal frailty and the inability to continue coping with independent living. Many people decide for themselves to go into a home, although with the full support of their family, carers and interested professionals, but for others residential care seems to be forced upon them. Relatives or carers who are unable to cope, or elderly people who have no such close support, could find themselves in a situation where their consent is never directly sought, but taken for granted, being 'the best for all concerned'. Conversely, consent may be effectively denied in another way, when the mere existence of a 'carer' could mean that someone is not offered the option of residential living.

4.30 Elderly people suffering from some form of dementia may be misled or simply not fully informed, on the assumption that they would not be able to understand fully what is happening to them.

4.31 Similar problems exist in respect of consent to medical treatment (See Section Two, Chapter Four). Obviously in an emergency situation doctors are justified in obtaining 'consent' from someone other than the patient but in many other circumstances, particularly when elderly people are extremely frail, whether mentally or physically, medical treatment may be pressed upon them for reasons that are difficult to justify if they are unwilling to be 'ministered to'. If elderly people refuse treatment, it may be assumed that they are unable to appreciate its potential benefit, rather than that they do not wish to be 'cured'.

4.32 In such cases, *de facto* consent may not be actively sought but simply implied on the grounds that it will benefit the individual.

4.33 In emergencies, when the patient is unconscious or otherwise unable to express consent, doctors may provide treatment without consulting third parties on the basis of 'necessity' (or the implied consent of the patient). Consent of a parent in relation to a child is now necessary only if the child does not have the capacity or maturity to decide for him/herself.[10]

4.34 In other circumstances the 'good of the many' may be an argument for dispensing with the consent of the individual. This may arise in the use of vulnerable elderly people by the media. If people suffering from senile dementia are shown on television in a way that they would probably have considered unacceptable in earlier life, can this be justified? Is the 'public good' i.e. the improvement in care which such exposure might help to achieve, sufficient reason to dispense with valid consent? In other countries, such as Canada, institutions have consent forms which have to be approved by a relative. It might be possible to develop a similar form in this country. Nominated representatives could, in the absence of close family, perhaps be involved in decisions about such matters.

4.35 Society generally and individual families are often loath to allow vulnerable people to exercise their full right to consent.

---

[10] See Gillick v West Norfolk & Wisbech Area Health Authority and the DHSS (House of Lords: Times Law Report, 18th October, 1985)

This is central to the issue of old age abuse (See Section Two, Chapter One). Elderly people subjected to physical violence may refuse to make a complaint or to leave their home. Frequently they are simply unwilling to criticize and draw attention to a son or daughter who may be unable to cope with an extremely stressful and difficult situation in caring continuously for them.

4.36 Most people in such circumstances are not willing victims. If, however, they refuse intervention and help, does it mean that they are, in fact, 'consenting' to this violence? They may feel that the implications of making an official complaint, together with the shame and possible consequences, would be far worse than doing nothing about it. They may be threatened and consequently are too frightened to seek help. In these circumstances, can it be justified to override their implied consent to the abuse in order to remove them from the place where it occurs? This might only be for a period of respite or assessment or to allow the introduction of medical or social services. The line between protection and representation is a very delicate one to draw in such circumstances.

4.37 One particularly problematic question is that of 'anticipated consent' or the 'living will' (See Section Two, Chapter Five). Its protagonists see it as a way of ensuring that a person's present wishes and/or entitlement to refuse treatment are carried forward and used at a time when s/he is no longer capable of making such a decision. If such a proposal were to be adopted it would be essential for the 'representation' of a person's present wishes to be balanced by 'protective' measures strong enough to avoid the risks of future abuse and exploitation. Further public debate on this is essential.

4.38 There are certain similarities between the Enduring Power of Attorney and the living will. Both are about circumstances which will change. One significant difference is that the Enduring Power of Attorney concentrates on the *property* of an individual whilst the living will is about action to the *person* concerned, although both assume intervening mental incapacity. The living will records a decision made on a specific date in advance of the changing circumstances whereas the Enduring Power of Attorney entrusts to another person the power to make the decision in the future, in the light of evidence at that time. A study of the living will is currently being undertaken by a small working party and its conclusion will be published in 1986 jointly by the Age Concern Institute of Gerontology and the Centre of Medical Law and Ethics, both at King's College London.

4.39   Denial of consent is an important feature of Section 47 of the National Assistance Act (1948) (See Section Two, Chapter Two). It allows the forcible removal from their homes of people who are considered to be at grave risk or to be a danger to themselves or to others.

4.40   Section 47 is rarely used, sometimes abused and is unsuitable in many cases. It is intended to be a protective measure, but it is in fact an abrogation of rights and individual liberty because it can be used to force people who are not mentally ill into an institution, where they will often remain for the rest of their lives. The onus should be put on the health or social services authority to demonstrate that it has tried all other appropriate means of community support and help before resorting to Section 47 and to review the situation regularly to ensure that people do not become unnecessarily institutionalized. Section 47 gives no guaranteed opportunity for representations by the person concerned or by carers or relatives. The situation is complicated by the fact that risk taking may be a danger not only to vulnerable old people, but also to the professional staff involved. They are the people held responsible in the event of a tragedy. They are, therefore, likely to be constrained in the degree of self-determination they will allow.

4.41   Through Section 47, vulnerable old people can find themselves compelled, albeit through genuine good will and a desire to improve their quality of life or even to prevent death, to act in a way which does not necessarily accord with their desires or carry their consent.

4.42   If people are entrusted to take difficult decisions regarding risk taking, it must be accepted that they cannot later be blamed if the outcome leads to tragedy. As a society we need to clarify our attitudes and support those to whom we have delegated authority to take such decisions despite the consequences, provided they are based on proper consideration of the circumstances.

5 THE CARERS

5.1 One group of people who are frequently overlooked when considering representation are the carers of elderly people. They are very often the people who first ask for support but then find themselves completely excluded from decisions once responsibility for full-time caring is taken out of their hands. The caring role is often not fully acknowledged. Carers have no right to be consulted and their responsibility and capacity for caring are often taken for granted. Not all people are able to undertake a caring task, and, of the great number who do, many cannot continue without support or training.

5.2 When action is necessary all those concerned should be consulted in advance. The prime consideration must always be the elderly person's wishes. This will often involve a case conference, which should not be restricted solely to professionals but should include involved relatives and carers.

5.3 In most cases where vulnerable elderly people are represented by others, it is by a member of their own family. The question arises as to whether these relationships need to be backed by legislation either because the elderly person may be 'abused' or the representative would feel happier to have a clearer role in law. The administration of any scheme which developed bureaucratic mechanisms would be very costly if all such relationships had to be included. Is such a safeguard necessary?

6 CONCLUSION

6.1 All the issues considered so far raise the dilemma of setting the infringement of individual liberty against the right to self-determination. All citizens living in today's highly structured society are subject to certain limitations in terms of their personal freedom. Any welfare state must be partly based on the assumption that interdependence and mutual responsibility are necessary and justified if everyone is to enjoy a reasonable quality of life. Vulnerable old people are undoubtedly one of society's more defenceless groups.

6.2   If one starts from the premise that under no circumstances may an adult who is not totally incompetent have his or her individual liberty curtailed or infringed in any way, then any proposals to reform present, or to introduce new, forms of welfare legislation are non-starters. An acceptance that some modification or extension to present legislative procedures may be necessary is basic to the argument that a group of vulnerable people are not adequately covered by the protective measures of which others have the advantage. Proposals that are intended 'to protect' vulnerable people presuppose an acceptance of some investigation of the circumstances which render them vulnerable. This in itself is to some extent an infringement of personal freedom.

6.3   Old people or their carers, in accepting some input from the health or social services, tacitly agree to a certain intrusion into their personal lives and to some assessment of their needs. A problem will arise if, after consideration, a proposed package of support or care is not acceptable to that old person and/or the carer, and if such a refusal leads to a situation of grave risk.

6.4   What, then, are the alternatives? If people are to be protected despite themselves, what are the minimal acceptable infringements of their right to self-determination, which society believes are necessary for their own well-being? Does the state have the right to make such an assessment of need, and, if so, how much will it be influenced by available resources and priorities? To what extent are vulnerable old people further disadvantaged by the paucity of legislation designed specifically to meet their needs? Should they be treated differently from other disadvantaged groups?

6.5   The most difficult decisions arise at the point at which all the less contentious steps have been taken and those responsible are faced with the quandary of deciding between inaction, which may mean neglect or further risk, or action involving an infringement of personal liberty. What should they do?

Further Reading

An Ageing Population, Family Policy Studies Centre, Factsheet No 2, 1986

The Elderly Consumer, National Consumer Council, 1982

Mary Gilhooly, 'Legal and Ethical Issues in the Management of the Dementing Elderly': University of Glasgow, M L M Gilhooly, S H Zarit, & J E Birren (eds): *The Dementias: Policy and Management,* Prentice Hall, New Jersey

Martin Lyon Levine, (Professor of Law, Gerontology, Psychiatry and the Behavioral Sciences, University of Southern California) *Rights for the Elderly in National Law Around the World*, International Centre of Social Gerontology, Paris, 1986

Sally Greengross, 'Campaigning and Advocacy': *Danish Medical Review* 1986; Kellogg Foundation: *Quality Asurance in Long Term Care.*

'Growing Older', (Cmnd 8173), HMSO 1981

Alison Norman, Centre for Policy on Ageing: *Rights and Risk*, 1980: *Mental Illness in Old Age: Meeting the Challenge*, 1984.

Population Projections, 1979–2019, OPCS, HMSO, 1981

Social Trends, 1986, HMSO

Strategies for Community Care, Association of County Councils, 1985

Anthea Tinker, *The Elderly in Modern Society*, Longman, 1984 (Second edition)

T C Twining, 'Psychology, Law and Mental Competence in the Elderly', in *Bulletin of the British Psychological Society*, Vol 36, pp 198–200, 1983

Alan Walker, *The Care Gap: How Can Local Authorities Meet the Needs of the Elderly?*, Local Government Information Unit, 1985

Age Concern Wants Action on Dementia, Age Concern Scotland, 1986

Dementia in Scotland – Priorities for Care, Strategies for Change, Scottish Action on Dementia, 1986

Section Two

CONSENT

Chapter One

Old Age Abuse

1 INTRODUCTION

1.1   The abuse of elderly people has recently been given some
prominence and attention by the public through the media.
Physical abuse is a criminal act and, through the existing
legal system, if there is sufficient evidence, prosecutions can
be initiated.

1.2   The limited work on old age abuse so far undertaken in the
UK, and research in the US, suggest that the victim is often
mentally or physically very frail and dependent.[1] Frequently
the victim does not wish to report this type of incident,
perhaps because of continuing dependence, or a wish to
avoid a public acknowledgement of family stress, or a fear of
being put into an institution. In extreme situations, the police
will prosecute without the testimony of the victim (e.g. in
cases leading to death).

1.3   Unlike cases of domestic violence towards young children,
incidents involving elderly people are dealt with on an ad hoc
basis by local authority social services departments, if
brought to their notice. As elderly victims may be mentally
competent, but unwilling or unable to complain, the
situation often closely resembles that of domestic violence
within a matrimonial or cohabiting context, except that the
elderly victim, for reasons of frailty or disability, is less likely
to be able to move out. In such cases, the cooperation of the
suspected victim cannot be taken for granted.

1.4   If a complaint is made to a local authority, there are no
systematic procedures or uniform national guidelines for
individual social workers to follow.

1.5   In cases involving children, social services departments have a *duty* to intervene and to investigate complaints. The British Association of Social Workers (BASW) has produced guidelines for use in cases of suspected child abuse (*The Management of Child Abuse*, November 1985). Social workers, however, have no right of access to the home of an elderly person nor powers to summon all parties to a case conference. There are no powers to remove an elderly person from home to a place of safety, other than through Section 47 of the National Assistance Act (1948), as amended, or through the Mental Health Act (1983), nor to arrange for an assessment. Health visitors tend to concentrate on preventive work with mothers and young children and have no statutory right of access to the home. It is misleading to think that many elderly people have direct contact with local authority social services. Only 3 per cent receive meals on wheels and 10 per cent have home helps.[2]

2 IN PRACTICE

2.1   The lack of knowledge about ageing and elderly people means that consistent practice is difficult to identify. At present, good social work practice is likely to involve intervention in three stages:

1 Gathering information about the client and carer/s.
2 Using a case conference to evaluate information and to plan intervention.
3 Follow-up action.

Social workers can offer advice, counselling, referral to emergency accommodation for the victim (often financed but not managed by the local authority) or referral to a solicitor and/or the police. In one local authority a social worker explained that in his area the procedure for a case conference for an elderly person would be based largely on child abuse procedure, and is invoked when working with elderly people in day and residential care settings.

---

[1] Christopher Cloke, *Old Age Abuse in the Domestic Setting – a Review*, Age Concern England, 1983

[2] *General Household Survey* 1980

2.2   Little can be done to protect vulnerable old people unless they explicitly ask for such protection, or are proved to be mentally incompetent, in which case there is recourse to the Mental Health Acts. The proposals in Section Five, Chapter Two of this report would, it is felt, be helpful in certain of these cases.

2.3   Focussing attention on old people who are vulnerable through chronic disability or mental or physical infirmity reveals a 'grey area' in law, between those people who are totally mentally competent, and those who may be vulnerable, often in the very early stages of dementia. Such old people may be even more vulnerable through being dependent on relatives who are themselves subject to extreme stress.

2.4   Should we not consider creating a framework granting limited powers of intervention to an appropriate body, following a complaint? Such a body would assess whether abuse was taking place, while not denying the right of the adult concerned to remain in a household at risk if determined to do so. The right of a 'consenting' victim to self-determination must be safeguarded, and it is also recognized that there will always be some difficulty in protecting people from the consequences of active intervention in whatever form. If any powers were to be given to an official body to intervene in family life in such circumstances, caring families would also need to have the right to help or resources to prevent such situations occurring.

2.5   Social services departments have very few statutory responsibilities towards elderly people, few powers to protect, none to represent them and limited resources to help. This is often overlooked when tragic situations are given extensive media coverage.

2.6   There is understandably great public concern about child abuse and social services departments work within a legal framework in such cases, according to specific guidelines. Even so they cannot always prevent tragedies from occurring. However in the case of old people there is no such legislation which can be used. There are as yet no family courts in which the situation could be dealt with more privately than in open court and there is no protection for victims and their families.

2.7　Social workers or other representatives of the social services department do not necessarily know who is vulnerable to abuse. Unlike the procedures for alerting the community health service about young children at risk, no one need ever know if a vulnerable elderly person is in a similar situation. There is a need to publicize those services that are available, whilst acknowledging that people cannot be forced to accept help if they are capable of making proper decisions.

3 ABUSE IN INSTITUTIONS

3.1　The abuse of vulnerable elderly people is usually assumed to be either physical or psychological ill treatment by unpaid carers – most frequently by members of the victim's family. However, it is not necessarily confined to those living at home, in the community. Deliberate ill treatment may also involve paid staff.

4 COMPLAINTS PROCEDURE IN INSTITUTIONS

4.1　Residents and their families are frequently reluctant or unable to complain to the managers of a home through fear of victimization or because there is no clear procedure. In local authority homes the role of local authority members and how to contact them needs to be explained. Volunteers could do much to clarify the procedure and might take on some further representational role on behalf of residents.

4.2　In the private and voluntary sector the Code of Practice, *Home Life* suggests that residents should complain to local authority inspectors.[3] The Nursing Home Handbook issued by

---

[3] *Home Life: A Code of Practice for Residential Care*, Report of a Working Party sponsored by the Department of Health and Social Security and convened by the Centre for Policy on Ageing under the Chairmanship of Kina, Lady Avebury. Centre for Policy on Ageing, 1984

the National Association of Health Authorities (NAHA) gives guidance regarding quality of care and standards in nursing homes. For the National Health Service, NAHA has issued guidelines for handling staff complaints about patient care, *Protecting Patients,* available through the hospital administrator or health service commissioner.[4] Vulnerable patients, their relatives or representatives could take similar steps if wishing to complain about ill treatment, neglect or poor care.

4.3 It is essential that residents, patients, relatives and representatives of vulnerable old people are given detailed information on how to complain, as well as assurances that their views will not be ignored and that they or the old person will not be victimized.

4.4 If residents or patients of homes or hospitals fall victim to abuse, it is difficult to see at present who would represent their interests if there is no family. This is a situation when an independent advocate or friend could act in that capacity, particularly as so many elderly people have no close relative to take on this role. (See page 129, para 2.4 for recommendations).

4.5 Staff working in residential homes and hospitals need to be encouraged to report incidents of suspected ill treatment. In addition a mechanism is required through which residents or relatives could express their concern without fear of victimization or ridicule.

4.6 Applicants for registration of a residential care home are exempt from certain provisions of the Rehabilitation of Offenders Act (1974) and have to declare previous convictions. The DHSS updates its records of all cancelled registrations and these are sent to each local authority four times a year. For children's homes, the department operates a 'consultancy service' to help local authorities involved in registration procedures. This service could possibly be extended to include all residential care homes.

---

[4] *Protecting Patients – Guidelines for Handling Staff Complaints About Patients' Care*, National Association of Health Authorities in England and Wales, 1985

4.7   Safeguards are equally necessary in respect of people offering respite care for old people. They already exist for foster parents and child minders. Families caring for very dependent relatives would be reassured to know that there was no history of assault, violence or dishonesty among paid helpers recommended by their local authority. It is also important that the criminal background of those seeking paid or unpaid work with vulnerable elderly people is checked. Applicants should be asked to disclose any convictions or cautions. This need not apply only to residential care, in all sectors, but to care 'in the community' where people can be most isolated and at risk.

5 DISCUSSION POINTS

5.1   It would be worth considering the following points as a basis for setting up procedures to help prevent abuse.

1 People should be made aware of both actual and potential old age abuse, its causes and ways of preventing it.
2 More systems of help, advice and support for elderly victims and their carers need to be provided.
3 Better ways of representing old people at risk of abuse should be sought and developed.
4 Better procedures for reporting cases of abuse or suspected abuse of old people need to be developed.

6 PROPOSAL

6.1   It is important to establish a mechanism, which is both preventive and protective, to avoid increasing the risks of abuse as more frail and vulnerable old people live into extreme old age in family or residential settings. Those caring for them need entitlement to some help and support. (See Section Five, Chapter Two Recommendations.)

Further Reading

Mervyn Eastman, *Old Age Abuse,* Age Concern England, 1984

Elder Abuse: The Hidden Problem, prepared for the House Select Committee on Aging, 96 Cons: 1st Session (Comm Print 1979)

Rosalie Wolf, Michael Godkin and Karl Pillemer, *Elder Abuse and Neglect: Final Report from Three Model Projects,* University of Massachusetts, 1984

Working with Abused Elders: Assessment, Advocacy and Intervention, University Center on Aging, University of Massachusetts, 1984

Chapter Two

Compulsory Removal From Home

1 INTRODUCTION

1.1   There is one procedure through which elderly people who are not mentally ill can be forcibly removed from their homes without their consent and placed in institutional care. This is estimated to happen to about 200 elderly people in England each year. The power to do this is given by Section 47 of the National Assistance Act (1948) as amended by the National Assistance (Amendment) Act 1951.

1.2   The Section's limited use raises many important questions about the right of an individual to do as s/he chooses and to behave eccentrically when measured against the general standards of society. The borderline between eccentricity and abnormal or anti-social behaviour is sometimes hard to draw. The Poor Law origins of the Act were closely linked to Public Health measures. Gray has drawn attention to the development of the procedure from a method of facilitating slum clearance.[1] In 1979 a survey carried out in the Northern Regional Health Authority gave some indication of what was happening.[2] Thirty-three people had been removed under Section 47 in the period 1975–78. The male:female ratio was one:three. Nineteen people were living alone and 31 were removed from their own home. Analysis of what happened to the people in this survey showed nine died within four weeks of removal and 32 (out of 33) had died within one year. This survey suggested that the use of Section 47 was declining, but acknowledged that some people might have been persuaded to leave home by other means.

---

[1] 'See article in *Community Care* (pp 19–20) 8th March 1979 by J A Muir Gray.

[2] D P Forster, and P Tiplady, in *British Medical Journal*, 8th March 1980

1.3   It is estimated that up to 50 per cent of elderly people dealt
with under Section 47 are in fact mentally disordered.[3] The
suggestion frequently made, that every old person placed in
some form of institutional care under Section 47 procedure
could better be helped by recourse to the Mental Health
Acts, would mean that at least half of those people would be
defined as mentally disordered when they are not, with all
the implications of such a diagnosis.

2 PRESENT SITUATION

2.1   Under Section 47 of the National Assistance Act (1948), as
amended, adults can be forcibly placed in institutional care
to 'secure the necessary care and attention' if they:

1 are suffering from grave chronic disease or being aged,
infirm, or physically incapacitated, are living in insanitary
conditions, and
2 are unable to devote to themselves and are not receiving
from other persons proper care and attention.

Only 15 per cent of these people ever return to their own
homes and the average survival rate is about two years.
There is very wide geographical variation in the use of
Section 47. Some local authorities never use it, some use it
rarely.

3 HOW IT WORKS

3.1   Section 47 is now applied in two different types of
circumstances – one is when the person has gradually become
'at risk' through self-neglect over a long period and a crisis
has arisen, the other when a person has become seriously ill
but is refusing hospital admission. The medical officer of
health, now known as the community physician, is
empowered by the Act to certify to the local authority that a
person fulfilling the conditions defined above should be put
into institutional care 'in the interests of any such person . . .
or not preventing injury to the health of or serious nuisance
to other persons'. The local authority may then apply to a
magistrates' court for an order committing that person to

---

[3] M Green, *Geriatric Medicine* January 1980.

institutional care. The maximum period for such an order is three months, but it can then be renewed. Only after six weeks have elapsed from the making of an order can an application be made by, or on behalf of, the person subject to it for its revocation.

3.2 The National Assistance (Amendment) Act (1951) changed the requirement for seven days' notice to be given if the medical officer of health and one other doctor certify that the removal of a person without delay is necessary in his/her interests. If that condition is satisfied then an order can be made without the seven days' notice being given.

3.3 Further, the application can be made by the community physician if s/he is authorized by the local authority to make such applications, either to a magistrates' court or to a single justice. Under the 1948 Act or 1951 Amendment Act an order can be made in the absence of the person to be subject to it or of someone present on his/her behalf. An order made under the accelerated procedures provided by the 1951 Act has a maximum duration of three weeks, but during this period the local authority can apply for an order with a maximum of three months under Section 47 of the 1948 Act.

3.4 The procedure may help relatives and neighbours who are worried that an elderly person is in personal danger or a danger to those who live nearby.

'Miss B, a 65-year-old lady, had no relatives and lived in a tiny college-owned, terraced house in a university town. She became a recluse, not even leaving her chair. She was looked after by her lodger, a chronic alcoholic, who did her as much harm as good, but at least fed her. When her chair rotted beneath her, it was thrown out and another replaced it. Her room had been insanitary for a long time and the college had made several unsuccessful attempts to have her removed to renovate the place.

The crisis came when the lodger walked out on her. The social worker's attempts to introduce services were always refused. The GP called in the local community physician who arranged for removal under Section 47 and admission to a geriatric ward. There she was tidied up, given treatment for anaemia and encouraged to walk. She was discharged to a Part III home until the college had renovated her house, after which she returned home, very pleased with the outcome.

In interview, there were no signs of psychiatric illness'

social worker

Or it may be used to help in less urgent circumstances:

'Mr D was an elderly man who lived alone. He fell and broke his leg but just wouldn't go into hospital. I used Section 47 because I knew he was unwell, the home was becoming unhygienic and I thought he was a danger to himself refusing any treatment.'

retired community physician

3.5 In some circumstances insanitary conditions may provoke the use of Section 47, even if they are not offending neighbours:

'We had a 61-year-old woman who had six dogs and never let them out. The state of her house can be imagined. We decided she wasn't giving herself proper care and, as she was "aged and living in insanitary conditions", we took her into a home to clear up the house.'

hospital doctor

4 CRITICISMS

4.1 Criticisms have been made of the Section 47 procedure. These have been based on the difficulty of defining 'insanitary conditions', and on the need to protect the liberty of the individual. There are also problems in cases where there is a lack of evidence and where the objectivity of decisions made by professionals or others is hard to assess. There is wide geographical variation in the use of Section 47, suggesting that some local authorities manage without it. Some professionals see it as a 'left-over' from 19th-century style public health provision and refuse to use it.

4.2 One psychogeriatrician who has made a study of Section 47 reports:

'A 70-year-old man who did his own shopping and lived a fairly independent life frequently left the gas tap of his cooker on. Neighbours smelt gas and feared he might one day blow

*himself or them up. They complained to their local authority
who in turn approached his GP. The GP considered that his
patient was suffering from dementia and urged the district
community physician to undertake a Section 47. The DCP on
visiting the man refused to approach a JP for the necessary
documentation. This led to a heated exchange between herself
and the GP. It transpired that the gentleman had simply not
been used to the gas cooker and indeed had shown a
preference for electricity.'*

4.3 In some cases there may be a conflict between the need to
protect elderly people from unnecessary suffering and
painful death and the desire to let them live as they wish.
Pressure is put upon social workers and health professionals
to do something, as this case from a social worker shows:

*'Mr Y had lived alone for many years. Seen as something of a
social recluse, he was referred to social services by neighbours
who claimed he needed help. A couple of visits ascertained
that he was capable not only of making his own decisions but
used his "independent" nature to refuse home help, day care
and all the other resources society can call upon to "look after
its old". The case was closed though the neighbours were not
placated.*

*Two years later, the body of Mr Y was found decomposing on
the living room floor. He had been dead 10 weeks.*

*Police, neighbours, GP and the local press wanted to know
why social services had done nothing for this man. Why was
he left dead for so long? Whose responsibility? Who is
therefore accountable? The neighbours' concern had been
vindicated, the agency set up and paid for to deal with such
matters was at fault. The local headlines the following week
said as much: "Old man left dead for nearly 3 months". An
internal enquiry at social services was undertaken, case notes
called for, social workers and GP interviewed. A report was
made to the social services committee. The coroner, though
determining a natural death, commented on the fact that an
old man could be left dead so long.'*

4.4 Professionals may be tempted to use Section 47 to protect
themselves from public criticism. They may accept it as a
'reasonable provision' rather than as a last resort, and it may

be used as a threat. Evidence suggests that the use of Section 47 depends on individual professional preference or policy in a particular local authority. Statistical information indicates that it is very rarely used.

4.5   There is no legal aid available by way of representation in court to people who wish to oppose an application that they be taken 'into care' under Section 47 although they may be given advice under the 'Green Form Scheme'. This means that representation is denied to individuals who cannot afford to pay a solicitor, whereas the local authority has its own legal resources to call upon.

4.6   It could be argued that mentally alert people of whatever age have the right to neglect themselves. If there is evidence of a public health nuisance this can be dealt with under the Public Health Acts. Where elderly people live in unsanitary conditions, action can be taken under the 1936 and 1961 Public Health Acts in England and Wales to clear up the home and, when necessary, a short stay arranged in a residential home for this purpose, if agreed.

4.7   The following case, from a social services department, illustrates the practical difficulties of trying to fit individual needs into the existing legislative framework and to reconcile the conflict between the refusal to use unsatisfactory procedures and the vulnerability of some elderly people, who may be dependent and at risk. This social services department has a policy not to use Section 47 and illustrates an area of disagreement among individual professional practitioners.

'Elderly spinster, 80, lived alone. She was referred to social services by the local psychiatric day centre unit which she attended five days per week.

At the time of the referral she had arrived at the unit with a black eye and extensive bruising. All that could be ascertained was that "a man did it".

Relatives living nearby were a cousin with a handicapped husband and the client's younger brother, whom, it was said, provided total support and would not allow any other people to intervene.

The cousin could only provide minimal support when allowed. Attempts to speak to the brother were frustrated by his reluctance to talk to a social worker. He became very abusive and threatened legal action against the hospital and social worker should his sister be put into residential care.

Although it was felt by all agencies that residential care was most appropriate, this could not be done as the consultant psychiatrist felt that she was totally unable to make a rational decision.

Since then there have been three further instances of bruising. The police have been involved but no action is being taken against the brother who has admitted that he could be responsible for some of the bruises, explaining that it is difficult to put his sister's teeth in when she keeps moving away.

He will not allow his sister to go into Part III as he feels that she is really in need of hospitalization. The consultant disagrees, saying that Part III is more appropriate as she is easily manageable, a point agreed by the social worker involved. However, Part III cannot be obtained as the client is unable to make a rational decision and because of the brother's attitude towards residential care. The current legislation has been looked at carefully:

Section 47 does not apply as, although she is 'at risk' and a danger to herself and others, she does not live in insanitary conditions. Also, this authority practises a policy of not *using this particular section.*

The new Mental Health Act does not apply[4] either and although both the consultant and this authority are looking at ways of trying to help, it would appear that this lady must remain in the community, suffering until she is either admitted to hospital or subsequently falls and is found dead.'

social worker

4.8   This case appears to indicate a lack of agreement about policy and practice between the various agencies involved.

---

[4] Mental impairment as a ground for guardianship includes 'significant impairment of intelligence and social functioning and is associated with abnormally aggressive or seriously irresponsible conduct'.

There is currently much discussion about whether Section 47 should be repealed, and in this particular case other options, such as a long term management plan, were apparently not explored.

5 DISCUSSION POINTS

Care at Home/Retaining Section 47

5.1 It has been argued that this section should be retained as it is used sparingly and judiciously, and is useful for the very small number of cases involved. In any event, alternative solutions to each individual elderly person's problems should be fully explored before Section 47 is used to impose on anyone a way of life which is not of his or her own choosing.

5.1.2 A higher priority must be given to support by health and social service personnel. Appropriate help, whether medical, social or domestic should be brought in as early as possible to help people remain in their own home. If there is a public health risk the Public Health Acts can be used.

5.1.3 If a person's physical or mental condition gradually deteriorates and circumstances put that person 'at risk' then s/he may well be known to health or social services workers. The problem may be due to insufficient domiciliary support or money to pay for necessary repairs or adaptations. Here the community physician could play a preventive role, and might be empowered to mobilize community provisions. If a person wished to stay at home but refused support, the community physician might have the power to direct a person to accept it. In each case, compulsion should only be a last resort. The powers involved should only extend to remedying particular problems, not reforming life-styles. A case conference should be held before Section 47 action is taken.

5.1.4 Where an old person has a serious illness or injury, a distinction should be made between those who clearly do not wish to die but fear going into hospital, and those who express the wish to be left to die. In the former, Section 47 might be appropriate as medical treatment could be of real benefit, e.g. treatment of a fractured femur or a burn. In the latter there is a tendency to assume that the patient must be acting irrationally because of depression and to seek compulsory removal or to force confrontation with the patient which may lead to withdrawal of cooperation. A positive decision to respect the patient's wishes allows for a plan to be made to provide care at home. This may mean mobilizing domiciliary resources and a continuing contract with the patient which would allow the situation to be kept under review.

5.1.5 It is also thought that Section 47 is inappropriate for the dying. What is at issue is whether a person has the right to live and die in squalor, or whether that 'right' should in certain circumstances be taken away by the need for protection.

5.1.6 When a patient has an illness or injury which is not life threatening, but is causing serious pain and/or will lead to long term disability if left unattended, a further problem arises. (A patient with a fractured femur is probably the most common example.) Compulsory removal in this type of case may be appropriate, but only where conservative management at home is impossible. In many cases a doctor will simply send his patient to hospital. Where the social conditions are satisfactory the hospital care provides an opportunity to deal with an immediate emergency while intensive domiciliary services are arranged. More use could be made of short-term residential care for the same reason.

The Reform of Section 47

5.1.7 All those who have conducted surveys into the working of the section conclude that, even where all other resources – medical, environmental and social – have been tested, there will always be those for whom some form of 'protective care' will be necessary. Section 47 could be redefined to ensure (See Section Five, Chapter Two) that (i) no one is committed to institutional care who could possibly be helped in other ways (ii) an elderly person has immediate right of appeal against an order, (iii) conditions are more strictly defined to ensure that no older person is left in an institution against his/her will after an order has expired, (iv) an old person can be given reasonable alternative options, such as sheltered housing or intensive domiciliary services, (v) a person wishing to return home should be given positive assistance to do so. No admission should be permitted without opportunity of legal representation and by inference Legal Aid – see Criminal Justice Act 1982 for parallel in criminal proceedings.

5.1.8   One option might be to build increased safeguards into the use of Section 47. Under the Mental Health Act, the Lord Chancellor is empowered to appoint 'visitors' for those people whose affairs are managed by the Court of Protection, though these are not involved in assessment (See Section Three, Chapter One). It might similarly be possible to appoint someone whose primary responsibility would be to represent the interests of anyone for whom Section 47 was being considered.

5.1.9   The British Geriatric Society (BGS) and the British Association of Social Workers (BASW) have produced guidelines for the criteria to be used in the definition of suitable persons and procedures to be used when Section 47 is considered.[5]

5.1.10 The BGS guidelines suggest that the criterion should be removal which will 'substantially improve their health'. BASW suggests that physically incapacitated people, living in squalid conditions could qualify if all available resources of health and social services had been offered and had been unsuccessful in improving the situation, and that, if the person was removed the situation would be improved in a physical and emotional way. They consider that in no circumstances should lack of staff and financial resources necessitate compulsory removal from home. If such recommendations were accepted, a method is needed to ensure that all appropriate alternatives were tried before resorting to Section 47, and that the responsible bodies could demonstrate that this had happened.

5.1.11 The BGS guidelines suggest that the correct procedure should be for a case conference to be convened by the

---

[5] *Services for Elderly People*, Guidelines issued by the British Association of Social Workers (BASW)

community physician, which involved all interested parties, before any decision was made.

5.1.12 BASW and others have felt that a qualified social worker should play a continuous role in the proceedings, including being present at the case conference, which should also, when appropriate, involve representatives of the housing and environmental health departments, and friends and family. They also suggest that a key worker should be appointed to explain to the client his/her legal rights. It may be that this is another area in which informal voluntary patients' friends could operate. There could be a review within a month of operation and regularly thereafter.

5.1.13 The repeal of Section 47 would undoubtedly remove a threat to individual liberty. Section 47 has, however, another purpose. It is sometimes used to deal with the effect that insanitary or unpleasant conditions have on neighbours, whose rights also need to be considered, and who may find squalor deeply offensive and be rightly concerned about the risk of fire or vermin. There is a danger of viewing them all as interfering, hard-hearted trouble-makers and it can be difficult for outside professionals to reconcile conflicts of interest, especially as they are only likely to have intervened at the latter stages of a history of aggravation or conflict. It is also worth questioning whether environmental health officers are the best qualified professionals to deal with this type of problem, when medical and social factors often need to be taken into account, rather than simply the state of an old person's living conditions.

5.1.14 It must also be accepted that some set of procedures is necessary to protect professionals who make decisions in such cases from being at times unjustly held to account when something unfortunate occurs. (See Section Five, Chapter Two, for an alternative method of dealing with this type of situation.)

Further Reading

Sally Greengross, 'Protection or Compulsion', in *Journal of the Royal Society of Health*, 1982

Guidelines for Collaboration Between Geriatric Physicians and Psychiatrists in the Care of the Elderly, British Geriatrics Society (BGS), July 1983

Neil Leighton, Richard Stalley and David Watson, *Rights and Responsibilities*, Heinemann/Community Care, 1982

Mary Marshall, *Social Work with Old People*, Macmillan, 1983

J A Muir Gray, 'The Ethics of Compulsory Removal', in *Moral Dilemma in Modern Medicine*, ed Michael Lockwood, Oxford University Press, 1986

Elaine Murphy, 'Section 47 – Protection or Compulsion', in *New Age*, Autumn 1983

Alison Norman, *Rights and Risks*, Centre for Policy on Ageing, 1980

Tim Rayment, '. . . But Some Just Want to Seek Their Own Salvation', *Sunday Times*, 3rd November 1985

Frank Wills and Derek Stanley, *A Section 47 Observed*, Little Stoke Surgery, Bristol, 1985

'Woman of 83 Lived in a Wardrobe', *The Times*, 14th November 1985

B. Hoggett, *Mental Health Law*, Sweet & Maxwell, 1984

Chapter Three

Admission to
Residential Care

1 INTRODUCTION

'Most elderly people who enter residential care do so without any legal procedures being taken to secure their admission'.[1]

1.1 To go and live in residential care can be one of the most significant decisions taken by an elderly person. It often means moving out of a familiar neighbourhood and the loss of many personal possessions. It may mean changing a house or flat for a shared bedroom. Independence and choice may be greatly reduced. If an elderly person is not to feel rejected, abandoned or dismissed the decision to enter a home must be a fully informed one. A person has the right to accept or refuse the move.

1.2 Many social workers have been concerned that mentally confused elderly people are often in no position to understand what is going to happen to them, and there are no legal safeguards to ensure that the interests of the old person are given due consideration. The increasing proportion of elderly people in residential homes suffering from some degree of mental infirmity will undoubtedly be taken into consideration by the current review of residential care (1986), chaired by Lady Wagner.

1.3 Although there may appear to be wide differences between private or voluntary and local authority homes, many of the issues considered below apply in all sectors.

---

[1]Paul Brearley, Frank Hall, Penny Gutridge, Glenys Jones and Gwyneth Roberts, *Admission to Residential Care*, Tavistock, 1980

2 THE PRESENT SITUATION

2.1 In 1981, 1.2 per cent of retired people were living permanently in residential homes (local authority, private and voluntary) and approximately 2 per cent were in hospitals.[2] Three-quarters of the residents in local authority homes were aged over 85. Local authorities in England and Wales were given the power to provide accommodation by Part III of the National Assistance Act (1948), Section 21 (1). Such accommodation is now known as 'Part III'. The local authority must charge for it (Section 22).

2.2 In 1977, the DHSS and Welsh Office issued 'Residential Homes for the Elderly – Arrangements for Health Care', a Memorandum of Guidance to local authorities[3]. The Memorandum asked local authorities to establish agreed procedures for assessing elderly people's needs for residential care. It did not insist that this should be done, although the DHSS does have the power to do so. The result is extreme variations in practice between local authorities. In 1977 the British Association of Social Workers (BASW) and the Personal Social Services Council (no longer in existence) published *Residential Care Reviewed* which again considered allocation and admission procedures. There is no legal requirements for private or voluntary residential care or nursing homes to make an assessment of the need for care before accepting residents. Where homes, in the main voluntary, accept sponsored cases from local authorities, the authority makes its own assessment.

2.3 Most arrangements for admission to private residential care are made by relatives, some with the help of a specialist agency, but many without any advice and guidance. There is little information available to them on the 'consumer' rights of their relative, or what to look for when signing the contract.[4] The influence of relatives in securing a protective environment is now seen to be a major factor when elderly people move into private sheltered housing as well.

2.4 There is no standard contract for people entering residential

---

[2] *Elderly People in the United Kingdom: Some Basic Facts.* Age Concern England, 1985
[3] DHSS Circular HC (77) 25, LAC (77) 13 and Welsh Office Circular 117/77, WHC (77) 30 (under revision).

care in any sector. Such a document could perhaps be a prerequisite of registration, and provide protection for prospective residents, who would have an opportunity to consider the rights reserved by the home, particularly those related to asking someone to leave (for example, what would provoke this, and how much notice would be given). There might be a case for an arbitration scheme to intervene in particular cases, without prejudice to the right to litigation.[5]

3 CRITICISM

3.1   Attention is often drawn to the poor quality of assessments of the needs and circumstances of elderly people. Nicholas Bosanquet[6] suggests that there should be a statutory duty upon the health authority and local authority to make a joint assessment of a person who is being considered for local authority residential care. The British Geriatric Society (BGS) and the Association of Directors of Social Services (ADSS) recently agreed a statement that an assessment by a physician in geriatric medicine or a psychiatrist for the elderly is desirable prior to a move to residential accommodation or after an emergency admission. The DHSS made the following comments regarding the involvement of more disciplines in the assessment:

'It might simply involve nominated officers, acting on behalf of the authorities concerned, considering separate reports from a field social worker (or other members of the social services domiciliary team), the person's general practitioner and the nurse member of the primary health care team who had knowledge of the person, and where appropriate, a representative of the housing department. The help of a

---

[4] *Which? Report* (March 1985) and a small set of checklists available from the Consumers' Association, Castlemead, Gascoyne Way, Hertford, SG14 1LH
Monica Wilson, *The College of Health Guide to Homes for Elderly People*, College of Health, 1984
Leonie Kellaher, Sheila Peace, Dianne Willcocks, *Living in Homes: A Consumer View of Old People's Homes*, BASE/CESSA, 1985
Jill Manthorpe, *Elderly People: Rights and Opportunities,* Longman, 1986

[5] Helen Bartlett and Rosalind Brooke-Ross, 'Terms of a Contract', *Community Care*, p 53 2nd January 1986. The authors point out that in West Germany there is a statutory obligation for a private residential home to supply a contract and believe that this should be the case in the UK.

[6] Nicholas Bosanquet, *A Future for Old Age*, Temple Smith/New Society, 1978

consultant physician in geriatric medicine or, for mentally infirm persons, a consultant psychiatrist, would be of advantage in confirming whether or not short-term hospital care could postpone or avoid the need for residential care.'

(See ref[3])

3.2 Emergency admission often precludes assessment procedures. Sometimes 'emergencies' account for almost half of a home's admissions. Often people are not re-assessed after admission, as their 'needs' are assumed to have been met.

3.3 It is important that thorough assessments are made. Vague concepts are used too often or people are classified incorrectly, for example as 'confused', 'depressed' or 'isolated'. Assessments can be highly subjective and imprecise and are often conducted by unqualified social work assistants in a manner that would be unacceptable when dealing with children or young adults.

3.4 It has been suggested that, as with the care of mentally ill people, specialist social workers should make assessments, but there are insufficient numbers of specialists (approved social workers) to deal with even the present requirements of mental health legislation. There is no equivalent qualification for social workers who wish to specialize in working with elderly people. Mental health training for specialist social workers is not designed to make them specialists in the problems of old age.

3.5 Even when there is a formal panel of professionals involved in admission assessments or a multidisciplinary approach, the role of medical practitioners is important. The elderly person's GP should be consulted, if only to confirm that a medical examination is advisable, or that there is an existing medical condition for which the person is being treated. Medical records are confidential so it is important to seek the elderly person's consent and to explain why the information is necessary. It may be that some local authorities should carefully consider their policy regarding payment to GPs for such opinions:

'We know that our local authority has ceased to seek GPs' opinions because they claim that they cannot afford to pay their fees.'

Age Concern worker

3.6 In the exceptional circumstances of an elderly person being under a Guardianship order (see Section Three, Chapter Two) some local authorities suggest that a GP and/or community physician should be members of assessment panels. The DHSS suggests that 'help' from consultants would be advantageous, although they do not expect the consultants to conduct examinations nor to make domiciliary visits. Though most consultants may be willing to serve on assessment panels, some may be unable to give time to this or be unwilling to do so, particularly if the procedure leads to more demand for scarce hospital beds.

3.7 The DHSS goes on to declare in the same Memorandum that 'undue pressure on the elderly person to undergo a medical examination, or to accept referral to a consultant is undesirable except in a medical emergency'. This is challenged by one eminent doctor who states:

'I feel strongly that a medical examination before acceptance for Part III should be mandatory. I am not sure that the presence of a doctor on an assessment panel is enough unless it is understood that such a person will make an appropriate examination.'

Letter to Age Concern England

3.8 There may be conflict between the reluctance of an elderly person to be medically examined and the desire for a thorough assessment to ensure an appropriate placement. A person's refusal to be examined must be respected. Under current laws, even a person placed under guardianship cannot be compelled to undergo a medical examination.

3.9 Good administration and practice in admission to residential care are essential. Elderly people should be able to visit residential homes before moving in, and be adequately informed and consulted at every stage thereafter. Good practice may be agreed as policy but not operate in practice. A contract between the resident and the home, delineating rights and responsibilities, would clarify the implications of entering residential care regardless of sector.

3.10 Greater equity might result from standardizing practice and procedures for admission to residential care. Local and health authorities have widely differing policies that stem from their own priorities regarding the allocation of resources.[7]

3.11 For elderly people who are mentally infirm admission is often dealt with by assuming their consent and/or approaching relatives. Consent may seem irrelevant to carers who can no longer cope. The real problem is often less one of obtaining consent than that a non-emergency placement in a hospital or a home cannot be arranged. Breakdown in family support is frequently found to be the precipitating factor leading to emergency admission which often results in permanent residential care.[8]

4 DISCUSSION POINTS

4.1.1 Informed consent to admission to care *should be obtained whenever possible*. An authority should be satisfied that the person has been given a choice of alternatives including services within the community.

4.1.2 A Code of Practice on admission should be drawn up by local authorities, clearly stating *the rights of residents*.

4.1.3 Admission should be considered by multi-disciplinary assessment teams or panels.

4.1.4 One local authority officer could be nominated to coordinate applications and admission policies. In authorities where decentralization is a policy, practice must be compared and evaluated.

4.1.5 The applicant should be visited at home and his/her daily life assessed. This should be a requirement except in emergencies.

4.1.6 It should be a legal requirement that qualified medical and social work staff are involved in the assessment.

4.1.7 Funds should be made available by the DHSS to investigate the wide variations in local authority practices. This might highlight the need for legislative review or a firm Code of Practice.

4.1.8 Special steps need to be taken to protect the rights of mentally disordered people before they are admitted to any form of institutional care. Where appropriate, a representative should be appointed to protect a person's interests.

4.2 There should be a medical examination before admission unless the person specifically objects.

4.3 Emergency admission to care should be followed quickly by an assessment of the old person's needs and wishes.

4.4 A clear, legally binding contract on admission should be drawn up to protect the rights and to detail the responsibilities of residents. It should include an explanation of what the home can do and in what circumstances a person would be asked to leave.[5] It should set out those financial or representational duties which staff are prepared to undertake (or who can take on such roles as advocates or advisers).

4.5 In general, a local authority should ensure that the procedure for admission to its residential homes is comparable to, if not better than, that required of voluntary or private residential care homes.[9]

4.6 Agencies offering the public a legal or consumer service should be prepared to take on the cases of very vulnerable people in residential care. Projects that offer isolated elderly people in residential homes a 'befriending' or 'advocacy' service should include people in local authority, voluntary and private care.

5 PROPOSAL

5.1 The above procedures need to be set out and followed and the wishes and interests of vulnerable old people safeguarded and protected on admission to residential care. (See Section Five, Chapter Two, Recommendations.)

---

[7] Joint DHSS/Local Authority Working Party Report *Supplementary Benefit and Residential Care: Report of a Joint Central and Local Government Working Party, 1985*. DHSS, 1985

[8] See, for example, the cases quoted by Counsel and Care for the Elderly in *The Crisis in Residential Care*, National Council for Voluntary Organisations, 1986

[9] See *Home Life: A Code of Practice for Residential Care*, Centre for Policy on Ageing, 1984, sections 2.1.1–2.1.8.

Further Reading

Paul Brearley, Jim Black, Penny Gutridge, Gwyneth Roberts and Elizabeth Tarran, *Leaving Residential Care*, Tavistock, 1982

Martin Cooper, *The Growth of Private Residential Care in North-East Essex – its Impact on Plans for Local Authority Provision*, Social Services Department, Essex County Council, 1985

DHSS Social Services Inspectorate Development Group, *Assessment Procedures for Elderly People Referred for Local Authority Residential Care,* DHSS 1985

L McDerment and S Greengross, (Eds), *Social Care for Elderly People: An International Perspective*, Social Care Association, 1986

J S Rodgers and J A Muir Gray, 'Long Stay Care for Elderly People: its Continuing Evolution', *British Medical Journal*, Vol 285, 11th September 1985

Chapter Four

Consent to Treatment

1 INTRODUCTION

1.1   Under English and Scottish law one person cannot touch another without consent. To do so is a civil wrong, or may, in certain circumstances, be a crime. There are, of course, exceptions to this, both in theory and in practice. The Mental Health Act (1983) allows certain compulsory forms of medical treatment. Physical treatment can also be given without consent in cases of necessity. This could happen if someone's life was in immediate danger, for example, or if a patient presented a serious and immediate threat to others.

HOW IT WORKS

Psychiatric Treatment

2.1.1   To be admitted to hospital and compulsorily detained under the Mental Health Act (1983), patients must suffer from some form of mental disorder and be in need of compulsory admission in the interests of their own health and safety or for the protection of others. The majority of all admissions (about 90 per cent), are not compulsory but 'informal'[1] which means that most mentally ill patients are admitted to hospital on the same basis as people needing physical treatment. In 1985, the Mental Health Act Commission reported[2] that there were 110,000 'resident' informal patients and about 6,500 patients detained under the Mental Health Act in England and Wales.

---

[1] Mental Health Act (1983), Section 131(1)

[2] *Biennal Report of the Mental Health Act Commission*, HMSO 1985

2.1.2 A person does not have to give positive consent to such admission. It is sufficient not to be unwilling to be admitted. Informal patients are free to leave hospital at any time subject to the holding and common law powers of doctors and nurses (for use in an emergency).[3/4] In almost every respect the legal position of informal psychiatric patients is the same as that of non-psychiatric patients. Both groups have the common law right to refuse treatment.

Consent to Treatment

2.2.1 Consent to treatment is rarely formally sought, except in the case of consent to an operation. A person's consent is usually inferred from his/her behaviour. For example, a person who attends a doctor's surgery and extends his/her arm for an injection implies consent to this ordinary and reasonable treatment. Consent to an operation is usually given more explicitly by signing a consent form before the operation. It is witnessed by the doctor who has explained the purpose of the operation. The doctor should not do more than s/he has explained unless it is an emergency (e.g. not do a mastectomy if the operation has been a biopsy). Sometimes if a patient wants to discharge him/herself from hospital against medical advice, a form can also be produced if persuasion by doctors and nurses fails.

2.2.2 Case law has not developed detailed doctrine in this area as it is rarely worth taking legal action over such issues. The patient, as plaintiff, would not only have to prove the point but also be able to demonstrate consequential loss to establish damages.

2.2.3 Doctors who proceed to treat without obtaining their patients' consent could in theory lay themselves open to actions for damages and, in extreme cases, prosecution in the criminal courts. An unconscious patient may be treated, provided the doctor has no reason to believe that the patient would object if s/he were in a position to do so, and when the

---

[3] Mental Health Act (1983), Sections S(2)(7)

[4] For wandering patients, physical detention may not be necessary. See, for example, the good practice identified by the Health Advisory Service in Northwick Park Hospital (Harrow Health Authority), as mentioned in their 1984–85 Annual Report (p 8)

treatment is urgent and cannot be reasonably delayed. This principle was established in a Canadian case, Marshall v Curry[5] which would probably be followed in the UK. The legal position is not the same for a patient who is conscious, however, when it appears that the 'necessity principle' would only apply when that person is deemed unable to appreciate the implications of what s/he is saying through impaired consciousness.

2.2.4 Valid consent to treatment usually involves three factors: (a) information about the treatment, (b) competence of the patient, (c) voluntary agreement of the patient to that treatment.

2.2.5 Two cases have been developed to deal with the problem of valid consent:

'The "*professional standard test*" has found favour in England and New Zealand and would probably be followed in Scotland. With this test, the doctor uses his/her professional judgement as to what to tell the patient, taking into account all the surrounding circumstance.'

Law Society of Scotland Course

In the case of Bolam v Friern the court emphasized that there were circumstances in which a doctor might choose not to disclose certain risks or features of treatment (in this case ECT).[6] It is suggested that this would apply particularly to confused or distressed patients, although there appears to have been more concern in this case with the doctor's, rather than the patient's, competence.

2.2.6 The case of Mrs Amy Sidaway concerned the giving of information about treatment she received in 1974, when she was aged 63.[7] Mrs Sidaway had an operation to relieve neck and shoulder pain. As a result she suffered damage to her spinal cord and was left partly paralysed. Mrs Sidaway complained that she was not told of the risk of paralysis nor was she given the choice of having the operation in the light of such knowledge. The House of Lords appeared, by a

---

[5] 3 DLR 260 (1933)

[6] 2 AII ER118 HMC (1957)

[7] Arnold Simanowitz, 'When Doctors Make a Few Choice Decisions on Your Behalf', *Guardian*, 14th November 1984

majority, to hold that, unless expressly asked (in which case s/he should always reply truthfully) a doctor's duty to inform a patient of the risks inherent in a proposed medical procedure depended on what was good medical practice, so that disclosure should not be withheld in circumstances where no reasonably prudent medical person would fail to make it. This appears (within rather extreme limits) to leave the resolution of the issue largely in the hands of the medical profession.

In relation to elderly people, the question whether a patient may have *asked* for information may be crucial. A confused person may express himself badly, or even be unsure about what is going on and hence what sort of things to ask about. Although the House of Lords did not expressly consider the issue, it may be that doctors should be put under some obligation to give patients the opportunity to ask questions, perhaps even inquiring whether they wish to ask them and, in the case of people with impaired faculties, to make positive efforts to ascertain whether there are things they wish to know.

2.2.7 In the UK a doctor is not obliged to disclose all material risks before obtaining consent. In other countries the test has become more 'patient orientated'. In Canada, for example, the Supreme Court specifically rejected the professional standard test (Reibl v Hughes, 1980). In some states in the US it has been held that consent should be based on all the relevant facts, or what the prudent patient would be expected to want to know (e.g. Canterbury v Spence, Federal Republic, 1972).

2.2.8 The charity 'Action for the Victims of Medical Accidents', (see Addresses on page 140) states that legal rulings are not as important as the recognition of a changing relationship between doctors and patients. It believes that a growing number of patients do want information about treatment and operations and that this can either be achieved by legal measures or by the education and training of doctors. Currently, patients should be told about the nature and purpose of treatment and about any serious side-effects. If patients want more information, they are entitled to ask for it and the doctor should answer truthfully.

2.2.9 The mental competence of a patient can cause difficulty when non-urgent physical treatment is required by a person who strictly cannot give valid consent. Mental disorder does not in itself make a person unable to give valid consent, especially as in many individuals competence varies over time and according to the nature of the decision to be made. In cases of doubt as to competence, a patient should be assumed to be unable to give informed consent but in practice this does not always happen. Few doctors want the delay involved in applying to court for an order, or think it necessary.

2.2.10 In 1986 the Mental Health Act Commission published a discussion paper *Consent to Treatment* which, together with the draft Code of Practice for the Mental Health Act (1983)[8] emphasized the difficulty of obtaining consent from patients whose mental condition limited the degree of communication by which they could be judged to have given proper consent. To overcome the most difficult cases, the Code proposes two options:

1 formally detaining all patients whose condition is adequately severe.
2 finding some other mechanism.

The first would considerably increase the number of patients formally covered by the Mental Health Act. It has been suggested that this would lessen the necessity of seeking consent in individual cases and would seriously affect the legal status of many elderly people, together with attitudes others have towards them.[9]

2.2.11 A decision regarding treatment is taken in what is seen as the patient's best interests by the *responsible medical officer*, the doctor who takes the final decision when judging the appropriate treatment. Such decisions are often arrived at by consensus within the hospital team, frequently in consultation with the nearest relative (although the relative's consent has no validity in law). There is a thin divide

---

[8] *Consent to Treatment* is published by HMSO (1986), the Code of Practice by DHSS (1985)
[9] See article by Rolf Olsen in *Community Care*, 6th March 1986, pp 24–25

between acting in the patient's best interests and acting
against his/her wishes:

*'When I was working on a bowel surgery ward we had an
82-year-old patient with cancer of the rectum. He knew this
and told us that he would prefer to have no further treatment
and be allowed to die. He didn't want to have a colostomy.*

*But the doctor decided he should have the operation. He got a
relative to sign the consent form by saying it was necessary.
The nurses couldn't do anything. We're not really able to
argue with doctors or stop a person being taken to the theatre.'*

nurse

2.2.12 In practice, many elderly people are admitted to hospital as
emergency cases and some have surgery without having
given informed consent. Obviously many cases are genuine
emergencies, such as intestinal obstructions, but many have
an elective element. For example a hip replacement
operation is not a life-saving procedure for most old people.

2.2.13 A patient may not be unwilling to accept treatment but still
be unable to give fully informed consent. An elderly
confused person, for example, may have an eye cataract
which could be removed by surgery. Strictly speaking it is
unlawful to treat such a person, except in cases of urgent
necessity, if the patient cannot give consent. In practice what
frequently happens is that, if there is agreement on the need
for treatment, it goes ahead. If treatment is offered it is
supposed to be necessary and appropriate for the
management of the illness or injury and is a matter of
discretion for the responsible medical officer. It is reasonable
for these treatments to be administered to an elderly
confused patient, despite the absence of consent, if the
patient is not unwilling to accept them. Explanations and
persuasion by the medical staff often achieve this. It is good
practice to ensure that the patient's relatives are fully
informed, though there is no authority in law for a relative or
responsible local authority to give consent.

'If people are confused we can usually persuade them. They
may say they want to leave because they are frightened of the
unfamiliar surroundings. We try and find out their fears and
reassure them.'

nurse

2.2.14 Relatives may be particularly important for elderly people who do not speak English. When there are no relatives or friends to help, an interpreter should be provided. Such services are sometimes already provided for young mothers.[10]

2.2.15 It is common practice in hospitals and elsewhere for staff to insist that elderly people take their medicine, even despite protestations that they would rather not. It is not only medical staff who get involved in the task of persuasion; sometimes relatives or even other professionals become involved:

> 'Last week two residents refused to take their injections. Perhaps in the short term it has very little effect but in a few months we would have major difficulties with them. So my task was to see them and persuade them that the best course of action was to accept the injections. The problem was sorted out in an hour and a half actual working time but if I hadn't been there, it might well have resulted in several hours later over a number of days.'
>
> Social Worker'[11]

2.2.16 *Home Life*[12] is very clear about the administration of drugs. It encourages residents to retain control of their own medication, if they are competent to do so, and states:

> 'Staff responsibility does not extend to insisting upon or making residents take medication.' (2.7.3) *and* 'Medication must never be used for social control and punishment.' (2.7.3)

2.2.17 Any discussion of the rights of vulnerable elderly people in this area needs to take into account the protection they are offered in research experiments. The law provides strong safeguards for children and the British Paediatric Association (see Addresses on page 140) has produced clear guidelines about protecting children:

> 'Children have their parents to look after them but the elderly patient living alone constitutes a particular problem. Even regular visits from a social worker cannot ensure that she will

---

[10] For more information on this topic, see: Alison Norman, *Growing Old in a Second Homeland*, Centre for Policy on Ageing, 1985

[11] Olive Stevenson and Phyllida Parsloe, *Social Services Teams: the Practitioner's View*, DHSS, 1978

[12] *Home Life: A Code of Practice for Residential Care*, Centre for Policy on Ageing, 1984

continue to follow the doctor's instructions, yet many such patients are entered into clinical trials to test drugs, say for arthritis, without being covered by adequate supervision and follow up.'[13]

Faulder gives as an example the case of an 83-year-old widow, Mrs Margaret Wigley, who was entered into a randomized controlled clinical trial to test a new drug. She died two weeks later. At the inquest, in July 1982, the coroner expressed concern that the trial protocol had not been strictly observed and that the patient's consent had not been sought. Ms Faulder comments:

'She was not told that she was in a trial, nor did she know that the treatment she was getting was experimental.'

2.2.18 Elderly people, whether in hospital or living in the community, need protection if they are vulnerable. Many elderly people are in a situation of dependency in relation to their GP. Consent to treatment given by relatives is not valid and sometimes this may appear harsh. The indignities of senile dementia may lead people to believe that anything is worth trying in the hope of curing or preventing it:

'Like many people I carry a bright red card with the word DONOR on it and it gives permission for the medics to use any part of my anatomy after my death. I would also like to be able to carry a card, obtained now while I am young enough to be competent to take decisions, saying that in the event of my living long enough to become senile and confused, the doctors would be invited to use me for any experimental treatment that might improve my condition or if not, help find methods of improvement for others.'[14]

2.2.19 In some countries legislation has been passed to deal with some of these issues. In the state of Florida in the US, the law guarantees specific rights to nursing home patients (Section 400 022 Florida Statutes)[15]. For example, patients have the right to be adequately informed of their medical

---

[13] Caroline Faulder, *Whose Body Is It?*, Virago, 1985

[14] Peggy Edwards, 'Viewpoint: Drug Trials with Elderly Patients' in *New Age*, Autumn 1983

[15] 'Complaint Assistance', Nursing Home Ombudsman, Office of Aging and Adult Services, Department of Health and Rehabilitative Services, Tallahassee, Florida 32301

condition and proposed treatment, unless otherwise indicated by their physicians, and to participate in the planning of all medical treatment, including having the right to refuse medication and treatment, unless otherwise indicated by their physicians, and to know the consequences of such actions. Patients also have the right to be free from physical and chemical restraints, except those restraints authorised in writing by a physician for a specified and limited period of time or as are necessitated by an emergency. They can refuse treatment from one particular doctor and request another. Medical records must be kept confidential if desired and patients can refuse to be used as subjects for teaching or research purposes. Florida has a Nursing Home Ombudsman Committee to which patients may bring problems or complaints. This can be contacted through the state's Health and Rehabilitative Services Offices or by free-of-charge (toll-free) telephone.

3 DISCUSSION POINTS

3.1 The increasing interest in self-help groups and in the prevention of disability and disease suggests that growing numbers of elderly people will want to be more involved and better informed about medical care. Communication between doctors and patients could be encouraged through appropriate training in the skills of listening and explaining. Personal choice should be recognized and heeded. The medical profession will need to react to growing concern about medical accidents, negligence and drug dependency, and to consider the issue of freedom of access by patients to their own medical records.

3.2 Problems regarding consent are not experienced by medical staff alone. Managers of local authority homes, private institutions and hospitals have to consider how far staff can be instructed to control residents or patients, for example by locking doors or giving sedation.[16]

---

[16] See 'Medication' (6.3) in *Inspection of Local Authority Care for Elderly Mentally Disordered People*, Social Services Inspectorate of the Department of Health and Social Security, 1985

3.3   One important safeguard might be to give people in residential care the right to retain the services of their own GP, whenever practicable and if the GP agrees. If there were to be a more standard form of contract for registered homes this might be included, or it might be an area which the local authority registration officers should take into consideration.

3.4   The issue of consent to treatment raises questions about the extent of legal intervention in every-day medical practice, such as whether the law should be changed to define more clearly legally valid consent. Consideration might also be given to introducing a system of some form of guardianship for people, with or without relatives, who are *not* covered by the Mental Health Act (1983) but who need the protection of an independent adviser. Should there be an independent organisation, such as the Mental Health Act Commission, which could monitor the treatment of elderly people who do not fall within the provisions of the Mental Health Acts?

3.5   The ethical questions raised by the issue of consent to medical treatment should be considered not only by medical practitioners but also by other professionals, such as social workers and residential home staff and by carers. They could also be taken up by relatives' support groups, now increasingly being formed around voluntary groups, hospices, social services departments and hospitals.

4 PROPOSAL

4.1   Some safeguards are needed to ensure that the valid consent to treatment of an old person is always sought, either in person or through a representative. An elderly person's refusal to have treatment should also be respected. The status of representatives also needs recognition as the consent of relatives is not legally valid. Such representatives' views could also be sought in situations involving research, portrayal by the media, etc. The proposals in Section Five, Chapter Two, by recognizing the role of carers and/or representatives, might help to avoid incidents in cases when there is some doubt about the validity of consent obtained or the methods used in seeking it.

Further Reading

William Bingley, 'Legal Eye' (article on medication and freedom of movement), *Care Concern*, Nov/Dec 1984

Civil Admission and Discharge, MIND Rights Guide No 1, 1985

Moral Dilemmas in Modern Medicine, ed Michael Lockwood, Oxford University Press, 1986

Gillick v West Norfolk & Wisbech Area Health Authority and the DHSS (House of Lords: Times Law Report, 18th October, 1985)

Your Rights in Hospital, MIND Rights Guide No 3, 1985

Chapter Five

The Living Will –
Anticipated Consent

1 INTRODUCTION

1.1   The 'living will' is the term used to describe a form of
'anticipated' consent, when someone who is rational and
competent to make decisions makes a written declaration
about what should happen if s/he becomes seriously ill and
for some reason, e.g. through brain damage or senile
dementia, can no longer consent to or refuse treatment. A
person, in drawing up this type of document usually
expresses the wish that in such circumstances his or her life
should not be 'artificially' prolonged by medical intervention.
The following is an example of a living will:

> 'It is my express wish that if I develop an acute or chronic
> cerebral illness which results in a substantial loss of dignity,
> and the opinions of two independent physicians indicate that
> my condition is unlikely to be reversible, any separate illness
> which may threaten my life should not be given active
> treatment . . .'

Such a document has no legal status in the UK. In a number
of states in the US, however, a living will is legally binding.
It is perhaps of significance that the Enduring Powers of
Attorney Act (1985) extends the legal power of an attorney
to manage the financial affairs and interests of a person when
that person is no longer competent to do so (See Section
Four, Chapter Three) but specifically excludes matters of
consent to or refusal of medical treatment, i.e. matters
relating to the person as opposed to the property of the
grantor of a Power of Attorney.

1.2   It has been suggested that signing some form of living will
would give doctors an insight into their patients' views:

'Patients should be encouraged to declare their own wishes in writing before reaching senility. There is appreciable concern lest increasing numbers are kept alive artificially in what (people) often refer to as a "cabbage-like" state'.

consultant in Scotland[1]

'A signed statement would have legal standing in the sense that it would be drafted within a legal framework to exclude the influence of any person who might have an interest in the early demise of the patient. However, it would not be legally binding upon any future clinician – it would be a statement of wish which would not necessitate any reciprocal commitment.'[2]

Views about the ethical questions involved in living wills vary as do opinions about the dangers and benefits of introducing them. For some people they would offer a dignified and autonomous choice in matters of great importance affecting their own person and an escape from paternalistic decisions determined by the differing views and beliefs of doctors. Many other people believe strongly that life must be prolonged whenever and however possible and that no-one has the right to refuse measures which might achieve this. There is also a widespread assumption that good medical practice does already allow people to die in certain circumstances.

1.3 The British Medical Association has expressed this last view. In its opinion, such a document would be irrelevant and unnecessary since it is possible for patients to die without pain. Its Ethical Committee fears that people could be pressurised by relatives to sign such a declaration:

'In reaching its decision, the Committee was concerned about the possibility of such a document which would have no legal status in this country, being accepted as a quasi-legal document which could, in its turn, arouse the fear in some people that they might, when partially disabled, be persuaded to sign such a paper by relatives or others. The Association's decision does not affect the current situation, in that any

---

[1] G S Robertson, 'Dealing with the Brain-Damaged Old: Dignity before Sanctity', *Journal of Medical Ethics,* Vol 8 pp 173–179 1982

[2] Ibid

patient may express his wishes, either orally or in writing, to his general practitioner, who will then be aware of the patient's wishes in this respect. [3]

1.4 The Law Commission of Canada suggested in 1982 that legally recognized powers should be given to doctors to decide whether to terminate or not to initiate useless treatment, starting from the principle that a doctor would act legally in not preventing death rather than illegally in not prolonging life, as at present.[4] While a living will might be useful in making a person's ideas and wishes known, it is recognized that such views may have been expressed because of misapprehensions based on misinformation or even through undue influence. There also remains the problem of what would happen if a signatory changed his/her mind once senility had been diagnosed. The time interval between the making of the living will and the event activating it would, therefore, be of crucial importance. In a minority (four out of 23 states which have such statutes in the US), there is a limit on the term of effectiveness of living wills.

1.5 Many doctors feel that misunderstandings surround medical practice when people are dying and that many people fear that their lives will be prolonged, even when treatment is blatantly futile. One case reported in the US in 1982 concerned an 82-year-old cancer patient who had spent the last months of his life on a life support machine. A number of American medical societies, including the Veterans' Administration who have 172 hospitals, have adopted a 'Do Not Resuscitate' policy for patients who have no reasonable hope of recovery.

1.6 Frequently, organizations concerned with the welfare of elderly people are dissuaded from discussing the issues raised by living wills. It is felt that the subject is too delicate, too complex, too personal or a mixture of all these. Many people hold contradictory views in this highly sensitive area. However, death and dying are a natural concern of elderly people, in particular, and many have firm views about the

---

[3] Letter from the British Medical Association to Age Concern England, (1984)

[4] Law Reform Commission of Canada, Working Paper 28 'Euthanasia, Aiding Suicide and Cessation of Treatment', p 69 (1982)

treatment they would wish to have in certain circumstances and about their future medical care.

1.7 Even if firm conclusions or recommendations cannot be reached, the subject needs to be more widely debated both to allay fears and to allow a more frank and open discussion of this highly sensitive and emotive issue.

2 DISCUSSION POINTS

2.1 Consideration should be given to setting up a body in the UK to consider these and related ethical issues. This has been done in the US and Australia, with the involvement of the mainstream churches.

2.2 A small working party has now been set up by the Centre of Medical Law and Ethics to study the subject of living wills. Its detailed report will be published in 1987 in conjunction with the Age Concern Institute of Gerontology, both at King's College, London.

Further Reading

George J Alexander, 'Premature Probate: A Different Perspective on Guardianship for the Elderly', *Stanford Law Review*, Vol 31 1003, July 1979

Handbook of Living Will Laws, 1981–1984, Society for the Right to Die (U.S), 1984

C Kart, 'In the Matter of Earle Spring: Some Thoughts on One Court's Approach to Senility', *Gerontologist* Vol 417 1981

A Keeffe, 'Living Wills Give a Different Perspective', 66 *American Bar Association Journal* Vol 914 1980

I Kennedy, 'Legal Effect of Requests of the Terminally Ill and Aged Not to Receive Further Treatment from Doctors', *Criminal Law Review* Vol 217 1976

R Lamerton, 'Why Not Euthanasia?' *Contemporary Review* Vol 92 August 1975

'The Living Will – Death with Dignity or Mechanical Vitality', *Cumberland Law Review*, Vol 163 1979

L Libow and R Zicklin, 'Penultimate Will – Its Potential as an Instrument to Protect Mentally Deteriorated Elderly', *Gerontologist*, Vol 440 1973

A Macdonald and G Dunn, 'Death and the Expressed Wish to Die in the Elderly: an Outcome Study', *Age & Ageing*, No 11, Cambridge University Press, 1982

M Mancini, 'Death with Dignity: Are Living Wills an Answer?', 78 *American Journal of Nursing*, 2133 1978

S Pressey 'Any Rights as to My Dying?', 17 *Gerontologist*, 296 1977

J Rachels, *The End of Life: Euthanasia and Morality*, Oxford University Press, 1986

P Riga, *Right to Die or Right to Live? Legal Aspects of Death and Dying*, Tarrytown, NY, Associated Faculty Press, 1981

N St John-Stevas, *Life, Death and the Law: A Study of the Relationship Between Law and Christian Morals in the English and American Legal Systems*, Littleton, Colo: Rothman, 1981

B Wootton, 'The Right to Die', *New Society*, 26th October 1978

Section Three

PROTECTION

Chapter One

Court of Protection

1 INTRODUCTION

1.1   If elderly people cannot manage their own financial affairs
because of mental disorder, the Court of Protection exists to
safeguard their interests. There has been some disagreement
about the exact numbers of elderly people suffering from
dementia, but its incidence increases with age and it is
estimated that 22 per cent of people over 80 suffer from it to
some degree.[1] Their vacillation and confusion, often in
relation to their financial affairs, can cause a great deal of
worry to others. Relatives, friends, neighbours and home
helps can feel vulnerable.

2 PRESENT SITUATION

2.1   The Court of Protection has existed in one form or another
for 600 years, but is now regulated by the Mental Health Act
(1983) and the Court of Protection Rules (1984). The Court
is an office of the Lord Chancellor's department but it is also
a court of law and has a judicial division consisting of the
Master, the Assistant Masters and other officers nominated
by the Lord Chancellor. The Court is authorised to make
orders and give directions in relation to the estates of those
who cannot manage their own affairs.

2.2   In June 1985, there were 22,545 people under the Court's
protection. It is estimated that some 75 per cent were over
60. Many live in residential homes or Part III
accommodation, others in hospitals or nursing homes, and
some in their own or relatives' homes.

---

[1] Alison Norman, Meeting Illness in Old Age: Meeting the Challenge, 1984

2.3   The Court's responsibility is for financial matters. It usually carries out its duties by appointing a receiver for the mentally disordered person (known as the patient). The work of external receivers is overseen by the Protection Division of the Court, and there is a Management Division which can look after people when no other receiver can be found, by acting as their receivers. The Court can authorize the receivers to do anything which the person him/herself could do if capable.

2.4   The application for the appointment of a receiver is normally made by the nearest relative of the person concerned. However, if the nearest relative is unable or unwilling to apply, another relative, neighbour, friend or business adviser of that person may do so, but the reason should be stated. The application may also be made by an officer of the local authority.

3 HOW IT WORKS

3.1   The Court may not consider that a receiver is necessary when an elderly person's needs are being met, and he or she has very few assets. These could be social security benefits, a pension, cash in the National Savings Bank, or a small insurance policy.

3.2   In other cases, if the assets are small or readily convertible to cash, but the person's needs are not being provided for, the Court may decide it needs to be involved. If the value of the assets is not more than £5,000 the first approach to the Court can be made by a letter or statement detailing the facts, and giving particulars of the person's assets and living expenses. A 'summary order' can then be made and no receiver need be appointed. This statement can be lodged by solicitors, a relative or friend, a local authority, or any other interested party.

3.3   If the assets are worth more than £5,000 but are still encashable in a simple way, the Court can make an order which will enable the assets to be cashed, withdrawn or realized in whatever way may be appropriate, so that the proceeds can be used for the person's maintenance or other needs, without appointing a receiver. In that case the question of whether or not a receiver is necessary cannot be decided by the Court until it has received an application containing full details of the person's means and requirements.

'I was in charge of the case of a long-stay hospital patient whose relative wished to gain control over her financial affairs for his own ends. His attempts to obtain an illegal Power of Attorney having failed, he was forced to go to the Court of Protection, whose procedures gave the hospital administration the opportunity to oppose the Receivership in the patient's interest.'

retired hospital social worker

3.4 When the Court considers that a receiver is necessary, the procedures differ depending on whether or not a solicitor is instructed to act. Generally speaking, the receiver, not the elderly person, will have to pay the costs of the solicitor for carrying out work which the receiver could do for him/herself but other costs come out of the person's assets and not the receiver's:

'Some receivers complain that they do all the work and cannot see why the sending and reading of an annual account should cause the Court to charge so much. I think the Court's annual charge is a strong incentive to relatives to try to obtain an illegal Power of Attorney. Perhaps the fee should be related to work done rather than to income, nowadays often needed for private care, if receivers are not to feel aggrieved.'

hospital social worker

3.5 Where a solicitor applies, s/he collects and prepares the appropriate documents and sends them to the Court. The hearing date is normally four weeks from the issue of the application. On the hearing, if everything is correct, an order is made by the Judicial Division of the Court appointing the receiver, fixing the amount of security which the receiver must give (which is effected by a security bond at the cost of the incapable person) and providing details of the maintenance of the person concerned and how his or her assets are to be dealt with.

3.6 Where no solicitor is instructed, the procedure is very much the same, except that usually the application is made by way of personal application through the Court, which gives the sort of help to applicants in filling out forms which they would otherwise get from a solicitor.

3.7 Once an order appointing a receiver has been made, the Court oversees the management of the estate and calls upon the receiver to account, usually every year, for his or her dealings.

3.8 It is expected that the receiver will normally make at least one visit a year to the person. The receiver will, in effect, step into the financial shoes of the elderly person and under the direction of the Court will do everything that a careful person would do for him/herself in managing his/her property and affairs. Administration continues until the person dies or recovers enough to be able to manage his or her own affairs.

3.9 An applicant who is aggrieved by an administrative act of the Court can call upon the Court to exercise its judicial function and can appeal from any decision of the Master to a judge of the High Court.

3.10 A commencement fee of £50 is payable on the issue of any originating application except where the clear annual income of the person is less than £1,000. There is also a transaction fee of a minimum of £50 levied in respect of certain transactions authorised by the Court, such as the sale of a house, and of £100 for an order for a will for the incapable person. An annual fee is payable, calculated by reference to the amount of the clear annual income at the disposal of the incapable person.

3.11 A receiver is required in most cases to file annual accounts of his or her dealings with an elderly person's affairs.

3.12 This monitoring process is intended to ensure that good receivers are helped and their burdens lessened, while bad receivers are identified, chased or replaced. Usually, annual accounts are requested for several years until it is quite clear that the receiver is careful and caring. At this stage, an annual enquiry might be substituted.

3.13 The Court can call upon the Lord Chancellor's visitors to assist in its work. The Lord Chancellor's medical visitors (who are consultant psychiatrists) can visit people with particular medical problems or to advise on the person's capacity to manage or make a will. The Lord Chancellor's general visitors visit many other people who are on their own or in a relative's home or a private, voluntary, nursing or residential care home. Visiting for the Court of Protection is only part of the general visitors' work as they are also attached to the court circuits as the welfare officers of the Lord Chancellor's department. Additionally, the Management Division of the Court has its own visitors, who make an annual visit to every person for whom the Management Division is receiver (approx. 2,582 as at June 1985).

3.14 Where the person is an in-patient an annual form is sent to the hospital. This will ask whether the patient is receiving all the clothing and extra comforts s/he needs, what social security benefits are being received, what balance of cash is held and whether this will be sufficient for the coming year, how much of the balance is available for investment and how often the patient is visited.

3.15 In normal circumstances, no visits or enquiries are made when people are in local authority residential homes because the local authority is expected to exercise its statutory duty to look after its residents' welfare and needs.

3.16 *Home Life*[2] recommends that where there is no-one else capable or willing to initiate the approach to the Court of Protection, the proprietor of a residential home should do so even though there is no legal obligation to defend the interests of residents (2.6.5). It says prior discussion with the registration authority about such cases is essential, and that:

'Under no circumstances should anybody connected with the running of the home be appointed receiver.' (2.6.5)

---

[2] *Home Life – A Code of Practice for Residential Care*, Centre for Policy on Ageing, 1984

[3] Though this may be less true nowadays; see, for example, an explanation of the work of the Court by its Master at a British Association for Service to the Elderly (BASE) conference in Cambridge reported in *Action Baseline* No 30, 1985

4 CRITICISM

4.1   Some people maintain that the Court has not made sufficient effort to acquaint people with its work, nor is there sufficient information in the training of key professionals, such as doctors, nurses and social workers, who may have to deal with the Court on behalf of their patients.[3]

4.2   There is often great reluctance to initiate referrals to the Court, even amongst those who know about it, because in the past applications took a very long time to process and there are still some criticisms about long delays.

> *'Mrs C was a very confused lady and was admitted to an old people's home with a reasonable amount of personal money. The money had been invested on her behalf by a brother who was also in his eighties and very confused. The family accountant and bank manager were co-operative but only had limited powers and the indication was that the application for Receivership would take too long a time for Mrs C or her brother.'*

local authority housing official[4]

4.3   Confusion exists about who is empowered to take steps to seek the Court's assistance, particularly for those without relatives, and where the person's financial means are either minimal or not really known.

4.4   The Court does not take responsibility for people with small regular sources of income or no substantial assets. Although it has the power legally to do this, the practice appears to have been discouraged and present levels of staff might not enable such an extension.

4.5   There is often criticism that fees are charged for the service of the Court when it could be said to be the state's legitimate function to oversee the affairs of those who are mentally

---

[4] See also, for example: Health Education Council, 1986 *Who Cares? Information and Support for the Carers of Confused People*, 'Carers who have used the Court of Protection have found it very costly, and say they would try and avoid using it if at all possible for this reason.' (p 36) and 'It is clear from letters which have been received that the expense and delay arising when the Court of Protection is involved is a source of complaint.' Alzheimer's Disease Society, *Introductory Booklet*, 1985 (p 12)

disordered. The size of charges has also incurred criticism.[5]

4.6   The jurisdiction of the Court can be invoked on only one medical recommendation, which sometimes gives insufficient clincal information. The Court's examination seldom goes beyond a single medical report and does not ask for a social report.

4.7   The criteria used by both the legal and medical professions to define 'mental disorder' and the incapacity to handle one's own affairs are imprecise.

4.8   Both legislative and practical procedures relating to the way the Court works seem to be based on the assumption that the people whose affairs are being managed understand what is happening to them, which may be totally untrue, and yet no legal provision exists to make sure that anyone other than the receiver represents the viewpoint of the people themselves (except following a specific application) when the 'incapable' person may be represented by the official solicitor.

4.9   It is unrealistic to believe that all such people would be able to exercise or understand their right to object to the Court's jurisdiction, yet the burden of raising an objection is put on the people themselves. The Court informs them that it is proposed to make an order appointing a receiver to manage their property and affairs, and objections and observations are invited by letter or telephone.

4.10   Patients do not receive copies of the evidence filed in support of the application or of the medical recommendations. Thus, even if they understand their right to object and choose to do so, they are not in a position to know the grounds upon which the application has been made until the hearing of their objection. This makes it difficult for them to refute the application or resist the Court's jurisdiction.

4.11   It is never right to assume that the person has little prospect of recovery or improvement, and the psychiatric and social disabilities of some elderly people can be alleviated by appropriate treatment and rehabilitation.

---

[5] Larry Gostin, *The Court of Protection: A Legal and Policy Analysis of the Guardianship of the Estate*, MIND, 1983

4.12 Not everyone is seen by the Lord Chancellor's visitors, even initially, because, in the Court's view, limited visiting resources are best devoted to people who are not already being visited by caring relatives or friends. Critics argue that a person's circumstances, health and needs can change and the Court should know. The Lord Chancellor's medical visitors made 1,396 visits (year ending 1st March 1984) and the general visitors made 1,434 visits (year ending 31st August 1984). The Management Division visitors made approximately 2,700 visits during 1984.

4.13 There can be difficulties in appointing family members as receivers. In a few cases a receiver with a vested interest in the patient's property may act inappropriately. There is a fiduciary duty to act solely on behalf of the person concerned but problems may sometimes arise where there is a conflict of interests. For example, it may be to the patient's advantage for money to be spent so she can return to the community, but the nearest relative, who is likely to inherit the patient's money, may resist this move.

4.14 The Court's staff of just over 300 civil servants is inadequate to keep about 22,000 cases under effective review and is incapable of developing its role. Based in London, it can appear geographically remote, distant and inaccessible to receivers.

5 DISCUSSION POINTS

5.1 It might be said that the Court is protective rather than judicial in its attitude to its 'patients' and that its practices are paternalistic. This may mean that elderly people are deprived of their right to a full scrutiny of their case consistent with the basic principles of natural justice. Or it could be said that it is too legalistic and not caring enough.

5.2 The Court could expand its information service to the general public and to all those coping with the practical problems of people who are mentally incapacitated. This would include giving guidance on tenancies, wills and the disposal of furniture and possessions.

5.3 The training of professional staff likely to be closely involved with mentally disordered people should include information about the Court of Protection.

5.4 Efforts should be made to assess the capacity of people to manage wholly or partly their own affairs. Therefore the Court should only be able to act on the basis of recommendations by two medical practitioners, one of whom should be a specialist in the treatment of mental disorder or a consultant physician in geriatric medicine. The procedure should be analogous to the requirement for civil admission to hospital under Section 26 of the Mental Health Act (1959) as amended by the Mental Health Act (1983).

5.5 A social report should also be obtained by the Court about the person's circumstances before an order is given. This would enable the suitability of a family receiver to be fully considered but would of course bring its own problems, such as increased expense and delay. If the local authority was required to produce the social report, would this have to be paid for? If the Lord Chancellor's general visitors were to do it, this would mean an expansion in their numbers at a time when the Civil Service is being reduced.

5.6 There should be provision for the notice of proceedings to be explained to the person by a social worker or other sympathetic person.

5.7 Where someone is incapable of understanding the procedure there should be a general provision to appoint an advocate or patient's friend who would consider the elderly person's viewpoint.

5.8 The Court should visit everyone who might come under its jurisdiction in order to ensure that there has been an adequate review of the evidence that the person is incapable of handling his/her affairs.

5.9 There should be regular medical and social reviews of the person's capacity to handle his/her own affairs and the suitability of the receiver.

5.10 The term 'patient' should no longer be used about those people who are clients of the Court, since it implies that they are all hospital residents. 'Client' is a possible alternative, or they might be termed 'wards', although this might lead to confusion with the much less common guardianship provisions of the Mental Health Act (1983) (See Section Three Chapter Two) and (because they are usually associated with children) might be thought to infantilize an elderly person.

5.11 Receivers should be obliged to visit the person at regular intervals and submit a detailed annual report, giving the Court an accurate and clear idea of the person's medical and social conditions, needs and quality of life.

5.12 Local authority residential homes or hospitals should not be excluded from a visiting procedure or an annual enquiry.

5.13 The possibility should be considered of making certain services of the Court free of charge.

5.14 One dilemma for the Court is that it has no power to make decisions about where the person concerned should live, yet it does control the finances which are likely to determine this. There is evidence that people with resources are directed to private care by local authorities.[6] In contrast, guardians can direct where a person is to live and/or attend for treatment. Perhaps this is why the combination of these two functions might appear logical, either by extending the powers of the Court to a welfare function, or by giving the guardian authority some financial powers.

6 ALTERNATIVE PROPOSALS

6.1 The Court of Protection could be the natural body to expand and to provide a caring role for all those who are mentally disordered and safeguard their quality of life. To do this its staff would have to be increased substantially and consideration given to regional offices providing a local service. Another way of extending the caring role of the Court could be through social workers attached to local

---

[6] See *Study of Assessment and Allocation Procedures*, DHSS South Western Region, 1975, by P Emy and D Lambert.

authorities or by voluntary advocates. Thorough training would be needed and the expertise of the Court's staff retained.

6.2   The Court's work could expand to cover the necessary administrative procedures for handling the affairs of people with only a fixed income and very few assets.

6.3   An expansion of the functions of the Court of Protection might provide an answer to the problem of protecting vulnerable elderly people. It protects some people from financial abuse but can it protect people's wider interests adequately?

6.4   The Mental Health Act Commission (1985) suggests that a power to manage property or money should be given to a local authority guardian (See Section Three Chapter Two) when the amounts involved are small. This would be more formal than the way in which nurses and social workers currently manage practical problems and less formal than the Court of Protection.[7]

Further Reading

The Incapacitated Principal, Report of the Law Commission, 1983.

Leaflets on the work of the Court of Protection are available from its office (see Addresses on page 140).

Jill Turner, 'Under the Lunatic Law', *New Society*, 19th January 1978

Dr Tony Whitehead, 'The Court of Protection', *Health and Social Services Journal*, 28th March 1980

---

[7] 'Biennial Report of the Mental Health Act Commission', 1985 (Section 8.15)

Chapter Two

Guardianship

1 INTRODUCTION

1.1   The Mental Health Act (1983) provided a mechanism in England and Wales whereby people over 16 could have their interests protected and be under some control. This is the Guardianship Order (sections 7–10). It is not frequently used. The Mental Health Act Commission estimates that less than 200 orders a year are made.[1] Powers can be sought to remove people from their homes under the Mental Health Act, either through their detention, which only allows removal to hospital under Part II of the Act, or by giving a local authority or another person guardianship powers. This clause makes no mention of place of residence and can be, and sometimes is, used to take people into local authority residential care homes.

1.2   When considering mental confusion, questions of definition obviously arise. Even if people are not diagnosed by a psychiatrist as mentally ill, they may be behaving in a manner that certainly indicates mental confusion. Some members of the British Association of Social Workers (BASW) feel that the guardianship procedures in mental health legislation might usefully be applied to elderly people who, although not suffering from discernible mental disorder, exhibit bizarre behaviour and a life-style that might suggest the need for a temporary appointment of a guardian. Other people feel that this suggestion is impractical and officious.

1.3   Others would argue that using mental health powers in all cases would be inappropriate, since the stigma attached to

---

[1] *The Biennial Report of the Mental Health Act Commission*, 1985, (section 8.5 (a) p 41)

mental illness is far greater than that of being unable to cope with everyday life.

2 HOW IT WORKS

2.1 To be received into guardianship, a person must suffer from 'mental disorder' as defined under the Mental Health Act (1983) and it must be necessary for the welfare of the patient or the protection of others. The application has to be supported by two doctors and made by an approved (qualified) social worker or the nearest relative, to the local authority. No application for guardianship can be made if the nearest relative objects[2] except by application to the county court. The guardian must be either a local social services authority or a person accepted by the social services; it is therefore effectively a social services order. A guardian has the power to require the patient to live at a specified place, to attend at places for medical treatment, occupation or training and to require access to be given at any place where the patient is residing to a doctor, social worker, etc. These powers are much less extensive than the powers of a guardian were under the Mental Health Act (1959).

2.2 Although a guardian can require a patient to attend a place for medical assessment, s/he cannot compel someone to undergo treatment without obtaining the patient's consent: thus guardianship patients have the same right as any others to refuse treatment.

2.3 A guardianship order lasts for six months initially. The first renewal is also made for six months. Thereafter renewals can be made annually. People placed under guardianship orders have the right to appeal to a mental health review tribunal and can obtain legal aid to pay for representation. Most often it is the local authority that applies for, and is granted, guardianship.

2.4 There are specific penalties against a guardian who ill-treats or wilfully neglects a patient.[3] The local authority can institute proceedings.[4] It can also start legal proceedings against anyone who obstructs an authorized person from visiting or examining a person under a guardianship order.[5]

2.5   If a guardian (other than a local social services authority) is performing his/her duties negligently and in a manner contrary to the interests or the welfare of the patient, the county court may order that the guardianship of the patient be transferred to the social services authority or to any other person approved for the purposes by that authority.

3 CRITICISM

3.1   The use of this Section of the Mental Health Act varies according to the policy and practice of individual local authorities. Many have a rigid policy of not using or not agreeing to guardianship in any circumstances, while others have no clear guidelines or procedures.

3.2   *'I have experienced reluctance to consider placing someone under guardianship of the local authority if the person is currently coping at home but I consider a breakdown is imminent. It would be useful to have the authority to move someone in an emergency. A demented 86-year-old patient of mine had an alcoholic cohabitee who repeatedly assaulted her. She was too confused to make a complaint to the police and I wanted guardianship powers to allow her to be removed from her home for her own protection if she were injured again. The local authority refused to contemplate this, suggesting that they might be held responsible for her injuries if she were on a guardianship order and still at home and they were only prepared to implement the powers if she were actually residing in their care.'*

hospital consultant

3.3   Problems have been raised by lack of clarity about the sort of client a social worker might think suitable for a guardianship order. Cooperative, compliant people would not need the safeguards. However, a social worker has no sanction against someone under a guardianship order who refuses to comply with directions:

---

[2] Mental Health Act (1983) Section 11 (4)

[3] Ibid, Section 127 (2)

[4] Ibid, Section 130

[5] Ibid, Section 129

'It is understandable, therefore, why some social workers regard guardianship as a waste of time.'[6]

3.4 There is a problem if a guardian considers that a place in a day centre, for example, is appropriate for a person and there is no place available.[7] Section 117 of the Mental Health Act (1983) imposes a duty (2) on the district health authority and local social services authority to provide 'after care services'. As Bedi reflects:

'It will be interesting to see how the courts interpret Section 117 when test cases are brought . . .'

This applies to patients admitted for treatment to hospital under Section 3 of the Act or under hospital order or transfer directions (Sections 37, 47 or 48) and then discharged.

3.5 The Mental Health Act Commission[8] confirms that some social services departments are reluctant to use guardianship because it might make demands on residential facilities or staff time. It has been suggested that guardianship is being used as a mechanism for putting people into institutions who might have preferred and been able to remain living at home.

3.6 For guardianship provision to be used appropriately it may be necessary to work out procedures and guidelines both nationally and at a local level. The initiative to use the powers appears to lie solely with social services departments. The role of community psychiatric nurses, specializing in psycho-geriatric work, may continue to become more significant, so joint agreements between hospital and community-based staff in both the health and social services need to be made.

3.7 Guardianship orders have most frequently been used to help people in the move from residential to non-institutional care, providing some supervision to help with the transfer.[9] A change of attitude is needed if more people are to benefit from guardianship instead of detention, says the Mental Health Act Commission.[10]

3.8 A guardianship has no power to compel treatment. The Mental Health Act Commission notes that this means some patients who would be able to live in the community if medication were obligatory cannot do so.

4 DISCUSSION POINTS

4.1   Clarification is needed to establish who can give valid consent, for example if someone in guardianship has an accident or needs non-emergency treatment for a physical or mental condition. Unlike guardians appointed under the 1959 Mental Health Act, a guardian now has no financial powers. The Mental Health Act Commission has suggested that this could be changed.[11]

4.2   Consideration needs to be given to the establishment of an independent organization to monitor the treatment of vulnerable old people who are not covered by the Mental Health Act but who require some protection.

4.3   Consideration might be given to a more flexible approach to guardianship and to its extension to people now not covered by the Mental Health Acts. However strong feelings regarding these Acts need to be recognized and their use in the case of people for whom they were not originally intended might increase their stigmatizing effect. Guardian-type procedures, however, might be developed to help certain vulnerable old people.

4.4   The draft Code of Practice for the Mental Health Act (1983)[12] which has been produced by the Mental Health Act Commission for the Secretary of State for Social Services, raises a number of points about guardianship. It suggests the option of guardianship should be considered more frequently and urges local social services departments to draw up guidelines about their arrangements for dealing with guardianship applications.

4.5   If the use of guardianship were extended consideration might be given to the potential role of guardians not employed

[6] Ben Bedi, 'Coping with Power', *Social Work Today*, 11th February 1985, pp 16–19

[7] Ibid

[8] *The Biennial Report of the Mental Health Act Commission*, 1985, 8.5 (a) (iii)

[9] Ibid, 8.5 (b)

[10] Ibid, 8.5 (a) (ii), see also section 8.12

[11] Ibid, 8.15 (c)

[12] Mental Health Act (1983), Section 118 – Draft Code of Practice. Published by the Mental Health Division, DHSS, November 1985

directly by the local authority. Could they be more effective if they were independent? How might they learn about resources which might help their 'charges'? Are there parallels to be drawn with 'guardians *ad litem*' of children in care proceedings?

Further Reading

Adriana Caudrey, 'Speaking Up for Children', (on guardians *ad litem*), in *New Society*, 1st November 1985

'Limited Guardianship: Survey of Implementation Consideration', *Real Property, Probate and Trust Journal* 544 (1980)

Jill Manthorpe, 'Guardians *ad litem* – New Plans Mooted', *Community Care*, 19th/26th December 1985. Report on Humberside Social Services department's development of a network to help guardians *ad litem* remain independent and well-resourced.

P Massad and B Sales, 'Guardianship: An Acceptable Alternative to Institutionalization?', 24 *American Behavioral Scientist* 755 (1981)

Grant H Morris, 'The Use of Guardianships to Achieve – or to Avoid – the Least Restrictive Alternative', *International Journal of Law and Psychiatry*, Vol 3, pp 97–115, 1980

REPRESENTATION

Overview

1 INTRODUCTION

1.1 There are various options for financial management which are examined in this section. They are: Agency, Appointee and Powers of Attorney.

1.2 Most elderly people have managed their own affairs all their lives and will continue to do so, but a minority will need to call upon someone else to help them manage their finances, either in a strictly limited or broader sense. In these situations they can become vulnerable to mismanagement, exploitation and a degree of abuse. Most old people are likely to live on small incomes as only a minority of pensioners have a good, index-linked, occupational pension; most others live on the state national insurance retirement pension, which may be augmented by means tested benefits or a small occupational or war pension. It is estimated that in 1981 810,000 elderly people did not claim all the supplementary benefit to which they were entitled by law.[1]

1.3 When today's elderly people were at work, incomes were generally lower than they are now and many people were unable to save for their retirement. Pensioners, particularly elderly women, who are likely to outlive men and be alone, often cannot afford the domestic conveniences that would assist with disability or frailty. Elderly people, especially owner occupiers and private tenants, are likely to live in homes built before 1919, which may lack basic amenities.

1.4 A National Consumer Council survey in 1982 found that 72 per cent of all adults have a bank account but this applies to only 57 per cent of women over 65.[2] This situation may change as more people are retiring either with a capital sum from their employers or with higher pensions, and banks and building societies are making efforts to attract them as customers.

1.5   The changing pattern of housing tenure is also significant. Over 50 per cent of retired people in England now own their own homes, possessing a large, if often unrealizable, capital asset. Thus many elderly people must cope with more financial and legal decisions than ever before.

1.6   As increasing numbers of elderly people own their own homes or have other income in addition to their retirement pension, there is a growing need for someone else to manage their affairs if they become mentally incapacitated. This does not normally present any particular problems, but vulnerable elderly people are open to exploitation. Financial management is usually undertaken by carers without the benefit of guidelines or assistance, and often causes anxiety.

1.7   The management of other people's money is fraught with legal and practical difficulties. Powers for delegating financial and other responsibilities are well established but little used. Some procedures do not appear to contain sufficient safeguards. Widely varying practices are followed by individual hospital, residential care homes, professional advisers and families. There appears to be a gap between what is practical and practised and what is legally correct. In fact, there is often no 'correct' legal procedure. When there is no law, the 'correct' position is even less clear.

1.8   In March 1986, the Social Services Inspectorate requested comments on new plans to simplify the arrangements whereby residents in Part III local authority residential accommodation receive their pensions. In the Inspectorate's view, the current system of signing agents is both expensive and risky in terms of potential abuse and theft.[3]

Plans which would involve a credit transfer scheme from the DHSS to the local authority seem to contain much good sense. The change proposed by the Inspectorate would appear to give local authorities the opportunity of ensuring that residents who want to manage their own money do so.

---

[1] Social Security Statistics 1984

[2] *The Elderly Consumer*, National Consumer Council, 1982

[3] *Social Work Today*, 24th March 1986, p 27

Chapter One

Agency

1 PRESENT SITUATION

1.1   If a person nominates someone to act on his/her behalf,
within given instructions, this person becomes an agent or
nominee. Under the social security system in the UK, a
person who receives a cash benefit may nominate someone to
act on his/her behalf; usually to collect the benefit from the
Post Office.

'Unlike appointment of an appointee, nomination of an agent
is not authorized by the regulations but is simply an
arrangement knowingly entered into between claimant and
agent.'[1]

The nominated person is called the *agent* and is just entitled
to collect the money, not to spend it or keep it without
specific instruction or authority. The duty of the agent is to
hand over the money. Thousands of elderly people use this
method to enable their family, neighbours, friends or home
helps to collect their pensions.[2]

1.2   The person entitled to the benefit from 'the payee', deletes 'I
acknowledge receipt of the above sum' which is printed on
the pension or allowance order slip, signs it as usual and
completes and signs on the back of the slip:

'I am unable to go to the Post Office and I authorize
.... to receive, as my agent, the amount due to me on
this order.' (signature)

This signature must be witnessed by someone other than the

---

[1] Section 9561

[2] For example, in a sample survey conducted in the London Borough of Wandsworth,
40 per cent of 222 recipients of home help service had their pensions collected by a
home help *Community Care*, 31st November 1985

agent. The person collecting the money, the agent, also has to sign the following:

'I am the authorized agent. I certify that the payee is alive today. I acknowledge receipt of the amount shown overleaf which I will pay to the payee forthwith.' (signature)

If this practice continues for 'a long time', as the DHSS term it, a card may be obtained from the DHSS (an agency card) stating that a certain named person, the agent, is authorized to collect the money for the payee. The payee still has to sign each order:

'You must sign each order due for payment on each occasion before your agent takes the book to the Post Office.' instructions on reverse of the agency card.

1.3 In the case of supplementary pensions, the DHSS now publishes a code of instructions to its staff known as the S Manual. One of its sections deals with the claimants who are 'unable to collect their money themselves' but are able:

'to complete a claim for Supp B, sign a declaration and notify changes of circumstances.'[3]

A *short-term* agent can be used if the inability to collect the money is likely to last only a short time. The claimant has to sign the receipt section of the Girocheque or order book and the form of authorization; the agent has to sign the Girocheque or order book foil in the presence of the paying officer at the Post Office.

1.4 A *long-term* agent is usually a permanent appointment but may be used if the need for an agent appears to be for some time. The S Manual states that interviewing officers should give a full report of the circumstances. The choice of the agent should be left to the claimant, though it is normal to appoint a spouse. Such an agent should collect all the benefits of the claimant, e.g. pension, war pension, etc.[4]

1.5 The S Manual states that staff should:

'Reconsider the need for an agent at each visit unless it is obvious that the claimant's condition is unlikely ever to improve and that the existing arrangements are satisfactory. If

---

[3] Section 9561
[4] Section 9569

it comes to notice at any time that the agent is not paying over promptly the Supp B due to the claimant, discuss alternative arrangements with the claimant at once. The claimant may request a change of agent at any time.'[5]

1.6 There is a special, though little known, provision for claimants who are temporarily too ill to be disturbed. If an agent has not been authorized to collect benefits, a 'statement of circumstances' can be taken from 'some responsible person' and the DHSS can pay 'for the time being, any person suitable, without taking permanent agent or appointee action.' They are instructed to obtain receipts.[6]

1.7 The DHSS also has a system whereby residents in local authority Part III accommodation can have an 'alternative agency'.[7] The local authority takes on the responsibility of cashing benefit orders on behalf of the residents. The claimant has to nominate as agent an official of the local authority (by office e.g. a senior official such as the treasurer, not by name). This agent, whom the DHSS refers to as the '*signing agent*', signs the order book and collects payments. A 'normal' agent does not sign the book as if s/he was the claimant.

1.8 The DHSS points out that in practice this means the pension order book is likely to be kept by the signing agent, 'so the claimant may be apprehensive about losing control of his pension'.[8] The DHSS instructs its staff not to press claimants to nominate a signing agency, if they prefer:

1 to draw their pension themselves; or
2 to nominate some other person under the ordinary agency arrangements.[9]

Claimants can still cancel or change their signing agent.[10]

1.9 According to a government survey of local authority old people's homes in London published in 1978[11] only five per cent of residents handled their own pension books. A small

---

[5] Section 9576
[6] Section 9590
[7] Section 9601
[8] Section 9602
[9] Section Ibid
[10] Section 9603
[11] *Residential Care for the Elderly in London,* HMSO, 1978

study of private and voluntary residential care homes in Bath (1982)[12] found that 38 per cent of residents retained control of their finances. It is suggested that very few homes consider that financial control by residents of their own money, however little, is important, in either practical or psychological ways.

1.10 The report by the Social Services Inspectorate on its inspection of local authority care for elderly mentally disordered people (September 1985) found that four out of five local authorities it surveyed in 1984 had a policy to take possession of *all* residents' pension books and to give them their statutory weekly allowance. 'It does, in the process, deprive more able residents of the opportunity of collecting their pensions in the usual way and maintaining control over their finances.' They found evidence that no mentally disordered resident received any money in some homes, while in other homes only one or two residents were regarded as incapable of dealing with money.[13]

1.11 The inspectors found that the money not given to residents was banked centrally and the interest accrued to the local authority in some areas. They found considerable variations in practice — in some homes relatives frequently helped mentally disordered residents to manage their money. In others, money was handled only by the head of home. In a few homes, some residents were encouraged to make choices and decisions about spending their money.

1.12 The inspectors called for general guidance about the most appropriate method of handling residents' money 'with specific guidance about handling the money of those who are incapable of dealing with it themselves'. Such guidance would appear to be long overdue if the varied practices they have identified (in an admittedly brief look at this complex area) are widespread. It would seem highly likely that

[12] Report in *Community Care* (14th March 1985) of research done by Stewart Greenwall, University of Bath which showed that out of six homes with a total of 230 residents, only 14 held their own pension book and ten of these were in one home. See also study of private and voluntary homes by Challis and Day (University of Bath, 1982).

[13] *Inspection of Local Authority Care for Elderly Mentally Disordered Patients*, Social Services Inspectorate of the Department of Health and Social Security, DHSS, 1985

procedures in hospitals were equally subjective and confusing. Quite rightly, the inspectors draw attention to the 'status' that possession of money may have for residents. To talk about 'pocket money' when a resident is receiving contributory pension is particularly demeaning.

Criticism and Comment

1.13.1 Very little attention is paid to the arrangements for appointing agents. Many people do not know the options. The DHSS does not produce clear information.

1.13.2 The system is largely unregulated so there are innate risks:

> *'I find repeatedly that people holding agents' cards regard this as a permit to sign the books themselves and I cannot tell you how often I have found that a patient is quite unable to sign her name but her pension is being regularly drawn by the agent'.*

social worker

1.13.3 Elderly people may be compelled by circumstances, such as physical infirmity or entry to residential care, to use an agent. They may be putting their money at risk and be unaware if their agent is regularly cheating them. If an agent misappropriates the money, there is no liability on the DHSS or anyone except the agent to make good the loss. It is the payee who must bear the loss if the agent does not refund the money or if legal proceedings are not successful.

1.13.4 The DHSS could help protect the interests of payees by increasing vigilance but this would present practical difficulties. One of the advantages of the agency system is that it is informal and flexible. Legal intervention to tighten the rules might protect some people but would be seen by many others as an intrusion and a complication.

1.13.5 It is essential that institutions keep proper accounts, particularly if staff act as agents. Ideally the money should be handed over to the payee before making any deductions. The proliferation of private homes for elderly people adds to the need for scrupulous practice, although the recommendations in *Home Life*[14] and increasing voluntary effort are helping to raise standards:

'Mr S was a 69-year-old man without any family. He was taken by Social Services to a home. His benefit was kept by the proprietors even though he had to sign for it each week. The DHSS paid the home £75 per week plus his personal allowance of £9.05 direct to the home. He was most unhappy there. He complained that at the most he received £4 of his weekly personal allowance. Eventually he announced he was leaving. The proprietors refused to give him his benefit book back, but he left. Mr S slept rough, penniless, then went back to Social Services to complain. After a while he got his benefit back but the DHSS paid four weeks' benefit to the home after he had left.

When he came to see me, I discovered that the DHSS had had suspicions about the home for some time and had known that no records were kept. No action was taken to reclaim the sum paid by the DHSS for the period Mr S was not there and the Department did not prosecute.

The man was fit and vigorous. He was prepared to leave and to complain. Many residents are frail and vulnerable and are totally unable to deal with such a situation.

I wrote an article about this case for a national newspaper and I have been contacted by a number of social workers who suggest this is by no means an isolated experience.'

solicitor

A recent survey in Norfolk[15] found that 38 per cent of admissions to private residential care homes were of people who received supplementary benefit.

1.13.6 In Belgium a personal account must by law be kept for each resident of an old people's home. It must be made available for inspection once a month by the person concerned or by the people or institutions responsible for the residents' welfare. These accounts may also be inspected by the relevant government department.

---

[14] *Home Life – A Code of Practice for Residential Care* Centre for Policy on Ageing, 1984

[15] Tim Weaver, Dianne Willcocks, and Leonie Kellaher, *The Pursuit of Profit and Care: Patterns and Processes in Private Residential Homes for Old People*, CESSA, 1985

1.14   *Home Life*[16] suggests that when the resident of a residential care home cannot find a relative or friend to act as an agent,

> 'the local social services department should be asked to recommend someone to act as his agent. The names of suitable individuals or organisations should be lodged with the registration authority.'[17]

It is unclear who will have the ultimate responsibility.[18]

1.15   It further suggests that proprietors or managers of homes should not be appointed agents 'unless it has proved impossible to find an alternative'. When this happens the Code says the social services department should be notified. However the suggested model (Annexe 3, Model 2) of a formal review/inspection check list does not cover this.

2 DISCUSSION POINTS

2.1.1   The DHSS should explain, in simple language, the role of an agent under its regulations so that both the elderly person and the agent understand what is entailed. Home helps, carers and other interested parties should be consulted about the practical workings of the system.

2.1.2   The computerization of benefits could make the detection of fraud or misuse easier. Where there is an agent, the DHSS should arrange for the pensioner to be visited so that any complaint or difficulty can be discussed.

2.1.3   A publicly available set of rules laying down how the nominee should act would help inspectors and managers to promote good practice. This could include guidelines for a system of monitoring and accountability.

2.1.4   Agency cards are inappropriate for people who are mentally frail. Agents should be informed of what to do if they know the payee is becoming mentally incapacitated.

---

[16] *Op cit.*, section 2.6.4

[17] Ibid

[18] Age Concern Berkshire are now running an advocate scheme as part of their agency with the local authority. Details of the scheme including selection procedure, tasks and guidance for agents, are available from Age Concern England. Details are also available from Age Concern Scotland of its advocacy action research project.

2.2 In any discussion of the role of agents who are not relatives or close long-standing friends, consideration should be given to extending the role of an agent to include some level of befriending and even some limited advocacy when appropriate. When it is not possible to obtain an independent agent, it is essential to build in safeguards if the proprietor or manager of a home continues to carry out this role.

Chapter Two

Appointee

1 PRESENT SITUATION

1.1   An appointee can collect, deal with and spend a social
security benefit:

'The Secretary of State is empowered to appoint someone to
exercise on behalf of a social security beneficiary any right that
the beneficiary has under the Social Security Act, and to
receive and deal with any sums payable.'

The S Manual defines an appointee as:

'a person appointed by the Secretary of State to act on behalf
of a claimant who is unable to manage his own affairs. The
incapacity may be permanent, e.g. because of senility or
mental deficiency, or temporary, e.g. following a serious
accident. The appointee makes declarations, reports changes,
receives and deals with any payments, and has a right of
appeal as though he were himself the claimant.'[1]

The statutory basis for this is contained in Regulation 26 of
the Social Security (Claims and Payments) Regulations 1981.
The beneficiary has to be 'unable to act for himself' and must
not be under the Court of Protection. An appointee acts on
behalf of and for the beneficiary. The relevant social security
benefit remains payable to the beneficiary when an appointee
exists. The benefit remains in the name of the beneficiary.
An appointee can also make the application to claim
benefits.

1.2   In the period 16th January 1984 to 13th February 1984 (one
working month) the DHSS recorded 3,898 cases of
appointments, making an average yearly total of 46,776
cases. This number includes a very small number of receivers

---

[1] *Supplementary Benefits: Procedure Manual*, DHSS, sections 9520–21

who act through the Court of Protection.

2 HOW IT WORKS

2.1   The appointee must apply in writing to receive the money due to the beneficiary. Social security staff are instructed to satisfy themselves as to the beneficiary's inability to manage his/her affairs. The beneficiary should be seen and, if this is not possible, appropriate medical evidence should be obtained. Appointeeships can be made for people of any age if they are mentally ill as well as for elderly people suffering, for example, from senile dementia. The power of making appointees is made by the representative of the Secretary of State for Social Services (an officer of the DHSS in practice) so there can be no appeal against his/her decision. The Secretary of State can revoke the appointeeship at his discretion. The appointee, who must be over 18, can resign with one month's notice and the appointeeship terminates if a receiver is appointed.

2.2   The DHSS is thus responsible for deciding who should receive and administer the money in the best interest of the beneficiary. Local social security offices have detailed instructions about the checks which must be made to confirm the suitability of the person who has applied to act. Prospective appointees should be interviewed to confirm their suitability. These interviews give an opportunity to clarify the terms of the appointment and ensure that they are understood. The DHSS cites illiteracy, frailty or confusion as features which might make it advisable to appoint someone else.

2.3   It is DHSS policy that a close relative who lives with or frequently visits the beneficiary is the most suitable person to act. This principle applies whether the claimant is at home or in hospital. If no close relative is willing and suitable, the appointee can be the secretary of the appropriate health authority, or a hospital administrative officer.

2.4   The DHSS notes instruct the appointee that 'any benefit you receive under this appointment must be used in the interests of the person named overleaf. If that person is in hospital you should ensure that from the amount of benefit you receive, a sufficient weekly sum is provided to meet the patient's personal needs'. (BF 57). Many people in hospital receive a reduced rate of benefit.

2.5 The S Manual instructs DHSS staff to be satisfied that:

1 the claimant is unable to act for himself in all respects;
2 the claimant will get the full benefit of the payments made;
3 changes will be reported promptly.[2]

2.6 It is the claimant's interests which are most important:

'Do not take appointee action merely, for example, for the convenience of the proprietor of a home when the claimant is able to understand the implication of claiming Supp B and what is required of him. It is important that someone acting as an appointee for several claimants understands that the portion of the claimant's income intended to cover his specific individual requirements, e.g. personal expenses, is not used for other purposes, such as being pooled into a common fund for the needs of all resident.'[3]

2.7 This is also brought out in instructions for bulk payments to organizations which act as appointees for large numbers of people. The money can be paid over in lump sums, quarterly, monthly, or in arrears, but DHSS staff should get an undertaking that claimants 'will receive their pocket money *each week*' (their italics).[4]

2.8 DHSS instructions to its staff are that they should:

'Check the case by visiting the appointee and the claimant at intervals appropriate to the claimant's circumstances.'[5]

2.9 In 1981, in England, 46,236 people aged 65 and over were living in hospitals for the care of the mentally ill and handicapped. Many of these people have the hospital as their appointee. When such patients receive supplementary benefit, if they are single it is immediately reduced. If they

---

[2] Ibid, section 9522

[3] Ibid, section 9523

[4] Ibid, section 9551. See also *Inspection of Local Authority Care for Elderly Mentally Disordered People,* Social Services Inspectorate of the DHSS, 1985 (section 4.6), which calls for "general guidance" about the most appropriate method of handling finances. (See previous chapter, p 99).

receive a retirement pension this is continued for eight weeks and then reduced by an amount calculated according to whether they have a dependant. After one year the pension is reduced each week but a dependant is entitled to the balance. If patients cannot handle cash or it is not therapeutically beneficial for them to do so, their benefit is spent on their behalf or put into their accounts.

2.10 Whether the appointee is the hospital or some other person, it is possible for benefit to be withdrawn or reduced to a 'reasonable' amount after the patient has been in hospital for one year.[6] The medical officer responsible must certify that the benefit cannot be used by or on behalf of the patient. It can also be done if there are substantial accumulations of benefit. The DHSS benefit officer has to consult the hospital staff and the patient's relatives, if any, to work out a 'reasonable' reduced amount.[7] In practice, authorities are reluctant to act in many cases.

2.11 It is not possible to be sure that patients receive their full allowances as statistics are not available. It is likely, however, that a large number of patients are entitled to, but are not claiming, allowances because they are particularly isolated and dependent.

2.12 An appointee's power does not extend beyond the handling of social security benefits. In practice, some elderly people who might be classified as unable to manage their financial affairs are not subject to the appointee system. If their income from supplementary benefit is sufficient to cover payment, the DHSS can arrange payment of their electricity and/or gas bills direct to the fuel authority. Rent, rates and water rates can also be paid to the authority or landlord. Such arrangements usually occur when arrears have built up.

'An elderly woman was referred to us by her GP who was treating her for mental illness. He suspected she had financial problems. We discovered that her gas and electricity supplies had been disconnected for non-payment of bills, so she had no

---

[5] Ibid, section 9538

[6] Schedule 2:2(e) of the Supplementary Benefit (Requirements) Regulations 1980

[7] Schedule 3:2(b) of the Supplementary Benefit (Requirements) Regulations 1980, No. 1399

*heat or light and could not cook. We brought this to the
attention of the DHSS as she was living on supplementary
pension. They awarded her the maximum heating addition
and put her on fuel direct – so the money to pay off her arrears
and for her current consumption is taken out of her benefit.
She didn't understand all this. Somehow she managed to buy
food but she hadn't paid a bill for years. Her rent is also paid
by the DHSS to the council direct'*

advice worker

Provision to take such action is to be found in Regulations 16
and 17 of the Claims and Payments Regulations 1981. There
is also the very wide-reaching Regulation 23 of the Claims
and Payment Regulations 1981, which enables the DHSS to
pay a claimant's benefit to 'such person as the Secretary of
State may appoint', if 'in the opinion of a benefit officer (the
claimant) is incapable of budgetting, or wilfully refuses to
budget, for any item of normal, additional or housing
requirements applicable to him.' This regulation cannot be
used if there is already an appointee.

2.13 In the above example, the person did not understand what
was happening. Such procedures and arrangements were
made informally and by personal contacts. Statutory
agencies may find it difficult to take such action, fearing an
infringement of personal rights.

*'Mrs C, who has great affection for a drunken, parasitic
lodger tenant, says that she wants to stay at home, but home
support actually means mainly looking after the tenant, who
steals her money and housing benefit cheques so that she is
liable for eviction because she has not paid the rent. She says
she would die without the tenant. Her son cannot get the police
in because she, he knows, would say that she gave the money
to him'*

research worker

3 CRITICISM

3.1 Although the power of appointee is obviously necessary and
seemingly innocuous and sensible, it does create some cause
for concern, as there is no monitoring of the appointee. In

some cases the system does not appear to work well from the start:

'Mrs W is a 90-year-old widow, living with her mentally retarded elderly son. I have been communicating with Social Security for them for about three years, filling in forms and writing letters on changes in their circumstances, because Mrs W cannot read now – she has macular degeneration and cannot write legibly – her hand shakes so much. However, she is quite capable of making decisions about her life and goes every week to collect her pension at the Post Office – walking on her son's arm.

'To my astonishment, some time ago I was made her appointee and sent her pension book. I never suggested such a procedure nor, despite letters, have they stopped sending it to me.'

Age Concern worker

This case illustrates a misuse of the appointee system since an appointeeship was never requested, no visits or enquiries were made by the DHSS and they have ignored requests to stop the practice. There was no need for an appointee as she could manage her own affairs and as she was able to collect her pension herself, not even an agent was needed.

3.2 *Home Life* states:

'. . . it is most undesirable that a manager or proprietor should take on this role whatever the pressures.'[8]

It suggests that the proprietor could seek a social services recommendation if no-one can be found. It is not clear what will happen if no-one is willing to act as appointee, except that the proprietor may be compelled to take on the task. This makes it possible for hidden extras to be deducted from the personal allowance with no safeguards.

3.3 As with social services recommendations on 'agents' it is not clear how much priority social services departments will give to recruiting suitable people as appointees and what their obligations will be to make sure the person recommended is

---

[8] *Home Life: A Code of Practice for Residential Care*, Centre for Policy on Ageing 1984, section 2.6.5

honest, competent and reliable. What checks will the social services department make, or will they leave it to the proprietor or DHSS to discover any problems? How much importance will registration officers give to liaison with the people they have nominated? These suggestions presume the existence of a fund of people willing and able to deal with the finances of mentally disordered elderly people. This may prove unrealistic.[9]

3.4   The DHSS claims that, for reasons of cost, it is unable to check that an appointee is acting properly. If the DHSS becomes aware that the appointee is unsuitable the appointment should be revoked immediately. Elderly people are dependent upon their appointees' honesty and good sense. Few abuses come to light but this may be because the elderly person is not able to understand fully what is going on and may trust the appointee unquestioningly. There may be no relatives or friends who, on behalf of the elderly person, could contact the Secretary of State, or his representative (the DHSS) about a misuse. Relatives can find their course of action limited:

'My father has been unable to work for several years and is now elderly. He was in a private home on the south coast but when his health deteriorated he went into hospital for a bit. I went to see him there and was told he had no money. The DHSS was paying the home his keep and personal allowance because the proprietor had been made his appointee. I went back to the home to pack his things. I found his only clothing was the stuff he had entered the home with and all the money said to be his was £2.

I find this extraordinary. My father does not smoke, drink or gamble. He rarely went out of the home, he had no holidays. In the period he was there his personal allowance would have amounted to about £550. I know my brother sent the home £15 to buy my father new trousers. I could not find any new trousers. No receipt was ever produced.

---

[9] See William Laing, *Private Health Care*, Office of Health Economics, 1985 which declares that 31 per cent of residents of private and voluntary residential care homes and nursing homes received supplementary benefit in 1984 to meet all or part of the charges.

The DHSS said it was not their concern, they had been sending the money and that was that. I know something is wrong.'

South London man

This case illustrates that there is no obligation to keep accounts. Individuals' money may be absorbed into so-called 'extras' or put into a group fund without trace. This misuse is hard to detect.

4 DISCUSSION POINTS

4.1.1 There is a need for more readily available information about the role of an appointee.

4.1.2 People who have their affairs managed by an appointee need to know what is happening and who to contact if they are unhappy or in doubt.

4.1.3 Appointeeship should be regularly reviewed by the DHSS. A form could be sent to appointees asking them to report any change in circumstances and to ascertain whether in their view the wishes of a particular old person are being met.

4.1.4 It should be mandatory for social security staff to see the claimants and for GPs to sign statements that appointeeships are necessary.

4.1.5 The DHSS should commission research to find out what is happening when the appointee system is used in institutions, hospitals, local authority, voluntary and private residential care homes. This could examine the experiences of local DHSS officers and their clients. As shortages of staff and increasing numbers of claimants have reduced regular visits, it is not known how often cases are checked, it at all.

4.1.6 When staff of homes or hospitals act as appointees, they should be obliged to keep accounts. The local authority or health authority should inspect these accounts. The DHSS should be able to inspect all appointees' accounts.

4.1.7 The inspectors of residential care homes should be satisfied that where staff or proprietors are the residents' appointees, they are acting properly. The DHSS, in liason with social services inspectors, should consider whether it is ever desirable for a proprietor to be an appointee.

4.1.8 Homes should clearly specify what their charges include and what are extras (e.g. soap, laundry). They should help residents use their personal allowance by arranging for them to have the opportunity to make purchases, go on outings, give presents, etc.

4.1.9 Hospital authorities, when appointees, should not be able to ask the DHSS to reduce or withdraw a patient's benefit.[10] The personal allowance should be used on the patient's behalf or credited to his/her account.

4.1.10 There have been suggestions that hospitals should be the appointees of all their patients. This would reduce the patients' independence and individuality. It would give patients little chance to make decisions and choices and could increase institutionalization.

4.1.11 Increased staff or volunteer time should be allocated to advising patients or residents who have difficulty organizing their own finances, but still receive a personal allowance. Independent agencies such as the Advocacy Alliance could possibly assist in this respect.

4.1.12 Vulnerable elderly people in hospitals or homes often have very little opportunity to take personal spending decisions and money may accumulate in their accounts. A greater range of services and facilities should be available to them. Appointees could review the choices open to 'their' elderly people and see how far they are consulted.

4.1.13 There should be no obligation to put patients' monies into so-called Patients' Clubs.

4.1.14 Some people who were admitted to mental hospitals before 17th November 1975 are not entitled to benefit (Transitional Regulations 12). They are provided with money for personal expenses by the hospital authorities – up to a maximum of £7.15. This exclusion of a small group of people is now anomalous and unjust. The Regulation should be repealed.

---

[10] Schedule 2:2(e) of the Supplementary Benefit (Requirements) Regulations 1980

5 KEY ISSUES

5.1   Agents and appointees will doubtless continue to work well for thousands of elderly people. Now may be the time, however, to tighten up parts of the system, particularly in the field of residential care and institutional care generally, to prevent the possibility of large-scale abuse occurring or being believed to occur. Appointees should be monitored and independent panels of experts should be appointed to visit, particularly when institutions act as appointees.

Further Reading

Disability Rights Handbook, published annually by the Disability Alliance Educational and Research Association.

Mark Dreyfus, Protecting the Mentally Incompetent; A Guardianship Tribunal, *Legal Service Bulletin*, No 8, p 75, April 1983 a short review of two Victoria government reports in Victoria, Australia.

Chapter Three

Powers of Attorney

1 INTRODUCTION

1.1 Since the Enduring Powers of Attorney Act (1985) came into force on 10th March 1986 there are now two forms of Power:

1 a Power of Attorney – described in paragraphs 1.1 to 3.7.
2 an Enduring Power of Attorney – described in paragraphs 4.1 to 5.6.

2 POWER OF ATTORNEY

Present Situation

2.1.1 A Power of Attorney is an arrangement by which one person (the donor) gives authority to another or others (the donee/s or attorney/s) to act on his/her behalf. The 'donee' of a Power of Attorney is required to act as if s/he were the donor. Decisions should be based, if possible, on the wishes expressed by the donor prior to becoming less able to deal with his/her affairs. The power can be either limited in scope to particular or to more general areas. The donor can still act on his/her own behalf after granting a power of attorney. There is an alternative of setting up a trust to manage income and capital assets. This continues to be valid, even if the person who creates it becomes mentally incompetent, assuming that person is not a trustee.

2.1.2 In practice a Power of Attorney consists of a legal document showing that the attorney has the power to act on the donor's behalf. It can be shown to those who require it, e.g. banks, pension funds or insurance companies. It should be kept by the attorney, who should provide copies of the document (not the original) when required. The donor can cancel the

Power of Attorney at any time. It is best to do this in writing and to inform the institutions or people involved. The attorney is required to take proper care of the donor's affairs. If insufficient care has been taken, resulting in a loss, the donor can sue for damages. The relationship depends on continuing consent and confidence.

2.1.3 A Power of Attorney cannot be created by a person suffering from mental incapacity. In law it is revoked if someone becomes mentally incapable or the donee becomes aware, or should have become aware, of the state of mind of the donor, who has become *non compos mentis* after the power was granted. The power becomes invalid and the donor's affairs should be handled by the Court of Protection, if appropriate.

How it works

2.2 In England and Wales a very short form of general (i.e. almost unlimited) Power of Attorney is found in the Powers of Attorney Act 1971. A document in this form allows the chosen attorney to carry out many legal matters on the donor's behalf. The Power of Attorney must be signed in the presence of a witness and sealed. Two or more people can be appointed as attorneys, a useful safeguard if they are appointed to act jointly.

Points at Issue

2.3.1 In practice, many attorneys continue to handle their donors' affairs even after the donors become mentally incapacitated.

'In practice, however, its operation is usually continued, unless a conflict of interest arises.'

Alzheimer's Disease Society

They may be unaware that in such circumstances the power is technically invalid, and people are often reluctant to go to the Court of Protection.

'We have certainly found that relatives who have continued to use a Power of Attorney even after the patient's affairs should legally have been vested in a Court of Protection order, have usually had the least problems and been put to least trouble.'
Adviser to carers

2.3.2 Relatives sometimes fear intrusion, delay or expense and therefore continue to act as attorney when the power is invalid. They may feel that, as the donor is physically declining, the situation will not last long. An attorney who continues to act despite being aware of mental incapacity may be liable for any financial losses incurred.

2.3.3 In some cases a Power of Attorney may even appear to be the only solution to a difficult situation.

Mrs H moved from a town on the south coast. She made all the arrangements for her removal but was in an obvious post-bereavement state, still feeling the presence of her husband and making provision for him. She had periods of confusion and bouts of hyperactivity. She deceived the DHSS as to the extent of her capital and thus received supplementary benefit. She was suspicious of her relatives and would not trust others with details of her money although she tended to boast about her resources. After a period of two years she became very weak and confused but no one could make arrangements to act for her. The home help felt very vulnerable in handling her pension collection as she feared accusations of misappropriation. Ultimately the solicitor and her adopted son made arrangements for a Power of Attorney and Mrs H was admitted to an old people's home, but it is open to question whether she was competent to give valid Power of Attorney.

field social worker

2.3.4 Elderly people wishing to appoint someone to look after their affairs, in the event of subsequent mental incapacity, cannot legally use an ordinary Power of Attorney for this purpose.

'We were told on consultation that this situation occurs commonly. An elderly person feeling that he is becoming increasingly less able to run his affairs efficiently, creates a Power in favour of his spouse or children in the expectation that they will use it to run his affairs for him. But a subsequent steady decline in his mental facilities is likely to have the eventual effect of terminating the power and frustrating his expectations.'[1]

2.3.5 A general, rather than a specifically limited, Power of Attorney may be too far reaching in some circumstances but

---

[1] *The Incapacitated Principal*, Law Commission No 122, Cmnd 8977, 1983

may be considered to be the only way of enabling one person to act on behalf of another. However it can lead to problems:

'. . . it may be that the grantor goes into hospital and later he or she may wish to return to the house, but the Attorney may have decided that the house shall be sold. The Principal has no recourse against the Attorney for selling the house in these circumstances.'[2]

2.3.6 There is no machinery for monitoring the role of an attorney.

'A client asked us to prepare a Power of Attorney for his mother whom we never saw nor had any contact with. We explained that she would have to be able to sign it and know what she was doing. He said that it would be alright and he took the document.

'We found out later that he had got her to sign it and gone round to the bank to make some arrangements. The manager asked him casually how his mother was and the son said that she had 'lost her marbles'. The bank manager said he couldn't then do anything with the Power of Attorney.

'So the son came back to get us to deal with the Court of Protection. He was furious.'

solicitor

2.3.7 Vulnerable elderly people in residential homes could be at risk of exploitation through abuse of these powers. *Home Life* emphasizes that:

'. . . in no circumstances should anyone connected with the management of the home be appointed attorney.'[3]

This is an important safeguard that should be enforced by inspectors of residential care homes and nursing homes.

3 ENDURING POWERS OF ATTORNEY

3.1 The Enduring Powers of Attorney Act (1985) came into force on 10th March 1986. It followed the Law Commission's Report *The Incapacitated Principal*[1], which concluded that better education about the limitations of the Power of

---

[2] Scottish Legal Action Group Bulletin, No. 60

[3] *Home Life: A Code for Practice for Residential Care*, Centre for Policy on Ageing, 1984, section 2.6.4

Attorney was not the answer to problems associated with the Power. The Commission felt that attorneys would not necessarily approach the Court of Protection in appropriate circumstances. It considered whether a solution might lie in abolishing the rule that mental incapacity necessarily renders the power invalid. The Commission concluded that this would be relatively simple and would accord with what many people mistakenly thought to be the law. To have done this would have legalized much current practice. It would also have removed the necessity of deciding exactly when a person became legally incompetent. Nonetheless, the Law Commission rejected this solution because it lacked safeguards and because a donor might not have wished the Power to continue once s/he could not revoke it.

3.2 The Law Commission recommended instead that the law be changed so that certain Powers of Attorney could continue after the donor became mentally incapable. These new powers were called Enduring Powers of Attorney (EPAs). The Law Commission tried to balance the need for a simple, effective and inexpensive method of allowing powers to continue despite mental incapacity with the need to protect the donor from exploitation:

> 'We have in mind the donor who is no longer fully capable when he grants the EPA, even though he still has sufficient capacity to create the power. This is likely to be a very common case in practice where (as will be most usual) the donor is elderly.'[4]

How it works

3.3.1 The Enduring Power of Attorney is designed to ensure that the nature of the Power is understood by donor and attorney. An Enduring Power can confer on the attorney general or specific authority to act on the donor's behalf.

3.3.2 If the attorney, under an Enduring Power, has reason to believe that the donor is, or is becoming, mentally incapable, s/he must apply to the Court of Protection to register the EPA. Before making this application the attorney must notify the donor and that person's closest relatives of the

---

[4] *The Incapacitated Principal*, op. cit.

application (Section 4 Enduring Powers of Attorney Act 1985). The Enduring Powers of Attorney (Prescribed Form) Regulations 1986 now prescribe the form and contents of the EPA.[5]

3.3.3 No order giving exemption from the duty to notify has yet been made by the Lord Chancellor, despite the Law Commission's proposals that the duty could be waived in certain circumstances. They gave as an example an attorney who was a member of a particular class or group such as a solicitor, a trust corporation, or a chartered accountant.

4 POINTS AT ISSUE

4.1 This new legislation will need to be carefully monitored as a safeguard against misuse. The Law Commission pointed out that the EPAs of some countries have less safeguards than they considered to be adequate. In Australia, Canada and New Zealand, amendments to recent similar legislation have been made in an attempt to provide adequate safeguards.

4.2 There is a tension between people's right to choose what will be done if they become mentally incapacitated and their protection against possible abuse. Despite its obvious advantages, the EPA still does not in itself resolve the problem of determining the exact point at which someone becomes mentally incapable. Medical definitions are still imprecise in this area. There is no requirement in the legislation for an independent medical diagnosis at the time of registration.

4.3 The problem remains of how to be sure that EPAs and Powers of Attorney are given without duress and are made knowingly. The forms are still difficult for an ordinary person to understand. The EPA Act and the regulations could be criticized because they fail to deal with specific points – for example if the witness is required to be independent or, additionally, is required to vouch for the donor's mental capacity and the fact that s/he appears to understand what is

---

[5] Court of Protection leaflet on Enduring Powers of Attorney, available from the Court of Protection (see Addresses, p 140)

being signed. It follows that vulnerable people could still be open to some degree of exploitation:

'I was recently aware that a Power of Attorney had been signed for a patient of mine requiring continuing care. In my view this patient was not mentally capable of agreeing. It was drawn up by a solicitor who acted as the witness. The Power of Attorney was given to the husband of the patient. He was the only other person present when the contract was signed.'

hospital doctor

4.4 Once registered the Court of Protection has the power to give directions on the management of the property and affairs of the donor, the rendering of accounts and the keeping of records, about which the Court can require information. It can also cancel the Power if, under Section 8 of the Enduring Powers of Attorney Act, the person is considered 'unsuitable to be the donor's attorney'.

4.5 Although Powers of Attorney are mainly concerned with financial affairs, the control they give of significant resources, for example, in purchasing various types of care in domiciliary or residential settings, may be crucial in determining the total style and quality of life of many vulnerable elderly people.

4.6 A relationship of trust is fundamental to the operation of an Enduring Power of Attorney. Many people would wish to appoint relatives as attorneys, but people can also turn to professionals such as solicitors or accountants to take on this role.

4.7 It is difficult to assess the effects of such recent legislation as yet and close monitoring of its use will be essential. Whether there are adequate safeguards against abuse of the EPA powers is a question that will only be answered in the course of time.

Further Reading

Journal of Social Welfare Law, November 1985, pp 344–50, contains useful criticisms of vague language in the 1985 Act.

Section Five

THE WAY FORWARD

Chapter One

Current Legislation

1 INTRODUCTION

1.1 In preceding chapters, several suggestions have been made for improvements and reform, some involving no more than changes in practice, others requiring some legislation. However, such measures would not in themselves deal adequately with the problems and situations described. More is needed. The following recommendations are intended to stimulate discussion that will hopefully lead to specific changes in legislation.

1.2 New legislation is necessary both to consolidate the best elements in existing law and to deal with new and changing circumstances. In conjunction with good practice, which any proposals should seek to enhance, such legislation should provide a framework which would secure certain rights to vulnerable old people and their carers. It would also ensure that their needs are considered and enable the relevant authorities to take appropriate action if and when necessary.

1.3 In reviewing present law specifically affecting the lives of vulnerable elderly people it may appear that existing procedures could be improved by piecemeal measures but such an approach is unlikely to provide an adequate long term solution to problems which will undoubtedly become greater as the numbers of very old people increase.

2 EXISTING POWERS

2.1 Under existing powers, local authorities and health authorities can, at their discretion, take certain steps to ensure that the interests of vulnerable elderly people are represented and that they are protected. The legislation is rarely mandatory and guidance on the extent of services is given in DHSS circulars. Such measures include:

2.2 **National Assistance Act (1948), Section 21, Residential Accommodation**
A local authority may provide residential accommodation for persons who, by reason of age, are in need of care and attention which is not otherwise available to them. This Section relates specifically to accommodation provided by local authorities who should have regard to the welfare of all persons for whom accommodation is provided and in particular to the need for providing accommodation of different descriptions for persons in need of such care. Local authorities are also empowered to make arrangements with private and voluntary homes for the elderly. Supplementary benefits legislation provides for financial assistance towards 'board and lodging' charges in residential care homes (other than local authority accommodation) and nursing homes.

2.3 **National Assistance Act (1948), Section 29**
Under this Section, local authorities are empowered to make arrangements for promoting the welfare of persons who are blind, deaf or dumb or who suffer from mental disorder of any description and other persons who are substantially and permanently handicapped by illness, injury or congenital deformity or such other disabilities as may be prescribed by the minister. Ministerial guidance as to the use of local authorities powers is given in DHSS circular 13/74. There are provisions in the Housing (Homeless Persons) Act 1977 (see para 2.7) and the Code of Guidance to the Act as to cooperation between local authority housing and social services departments in respect of 'vulnerable' people with a priority need.

2.4 **National Assistance Act (1948), as amended, Section 47**
Under this Section, adults can be placed in institutional care to 'secure the necessary care and attention' if they:

1 are suffering from grave chronic disease or being aged, infirm or physically incapacitated, are living in insanitary conditions, and
2 are unable to devote to themselves and are not receiving

from other persons proper care and attention.

2.5   **Health Services and Public Health Act (1968), Section 45**
This provides a power for a local authority, with the approval of the Minister of Health and to such extent as he may direct, to promote the welfare of old people. This was qualified by the DHSS circular 19/71, in which it was stated that, although the purpose of the Section was 'to promote the welfare of the elderly generally and, so far as possible, prevent or postpone personal or social deterioration or breakdown, until considerably more experience has been gained of promoting the welfare of old people, the Secretary of State has no intention of using his power under S 45 to direct . . .' There is no power to make direct cash grants (cf. Section 1 Child Care Act 1980). DHSS circular 19/71 in effect replaces statutory provision regarding meals and recreation for elderly people (National Assistance Act 1984 Amendment Act 1962) by giving approval to arrangements by local authorities for any of the following purposes to meet the needs of elderly people:

1 to provide meals and recreation in the home and elsewhere;
2 to inform the elderly of services available to them and to identify elderly people in need of services;
3 to provide facilities or assistance in travelling to and from the home for the purpose of participating in services provided by the authority or similar services;
4 to assist in finding suitable households for boarding elderly persons;
5 to provide visiting and advisory services and social work support;
6 to provide practical assistance in the home, including assistance in the carrying out of works of adaptation or the provision of any additional facilities designed to secure greater safety, comfort or convenience;
7 to contribute to the cost of employing a warden on welfare functions in warden assisted housing schemes;
8 to provide warden services for occupiers of private housing.

This method of legislating is unsatisfactory. It is difficult for the public to ascertain the precise meaning and intent of legislation; there is wide variation in interpretation; and no clear entitlement is created (cf. Chronically Sick and Disabled Persons Act (1970) which creates a duty on local authorities with a right, albeit limited, to apply for a direction from the Secretary of State to the local authority). Further, the circular relates the exercise of discretion to financial resources:

'The Secretary of State nevertheless recognizes that there are limitations of other kinds. The present shortage of staff, and the limited knowledge of the total needs of the elderly and how best to meet them, make it in his view both impracticable and undesirable for all authorities to seek to provide from the outset all possible services for all the elderly. It appears to him that it will be necessary (as suggested in later paragraphs) to lay down priorities both of recipients and of services, and to proceed by way of experiment and in stages to provide services of various kinds.'

It is interesting to note that although the circular recognized that the guidance given was 'necessarily in general terms' and it was hoped that 'it will be possible to give more detailed guidance in due course', no such additional guidance has, in fact, been given. The lack of clarity regarding entitlement is illustrated by the varied approach to adaptations in the home which are sanctioned by this circular, the Chronically Sick and Disabled Persons Act (1970) and also housing legislation.

2.6 **Chronically Sick and Disabled Persons Act (1970)**
Lays upon every local authority who has duties under Section 29 of the National Assistance Act (1948) the duty to inform themselves of the number of people within their area to whom this applies and to make arrangements for certain welfare services to be provided for persons in need.

2.7 **Housing (Homeless Persons) Act (1977)**
Section 2.(1) For the purpose of this Act a homeless person or a person threatened with homelessness has a priority need for accommodation when the housing authority is satisfied that he is within one of the following categories:

(c) he or any person who resides or might reasonably be expected to reside with him is vulnerable as a result of old age, mental illness or handicap or physical disability or other special reason.

2.8 **National Health Service Act (1977), Schedule 8**
Permits social services to make arrangements for the
prevention of illness, the care of persons suffering from
illness, and for the after-care of persons who have been
suffering from illness, including the appointment of mental
welfare officers under the Mental Health Act 1959 (para 2)
and places them under a *duty* to make adequate provision for
the needs of their area for home help for households where
such help is required 'owing to the presence of . . . a person
who is . . . aged . . .' (para 3). DHSS guidelines on the
provision of home helps (home helps per thousand heads of
the relevant population) are no longer issued. A recent
survey showed wide variation in practice. The implication
that the 'needs of the area' will be identified is difficult to
reconcile with the advice that is still current in circular 19/71:

'Experience suggests that attempts to compile a
comprehensive 'register' of the elderly are misconceived. No
scheme to identify the elderly in need of help should be
undertaken without full consideration of the purposes it is
intended to serve and *the expectation of immediate help which
may be aroused* (emphasis supplied). This consideration will
largely determine the form the scheme is to take . . .'

2.9.1 **Mental Health Act (1983), Sections 7–10**
As we have seen in Section Three, Chapter Two, the Mental
Health Act (1983) expanded the provisions of Section 7 of
the Mental Health Act (1959) to local social services
authorities. It has been suggested that guardianship powers
should be used in respect of people not suffering from mental
disorder as defined within the terms of the Mental Health
Act but who are confused and may exhibit bizarre behaviour.
This would not, however, eliminate the stigma of applying
mental health remedies to those for whom the Act was not
originally intended.

2.9.2 **Mental Health Act (1983), Section 117**
Under Section 117 of this Act, health and social services
authorities have a duty to provide for the after-care needs of
patients on discharge from Section 3 or Section 37 of the
Mental Health Act. It might be useful to give some
consideration as to whether this duty could be extended to
people on whom guardianship orders (Section 7) are made.

2.10   **The Registered Homes Act 1984** and regulations made under
the Act make provision for the registration and inspection of
residential care homes offering both board and personal care
for four or more persons. The regulations deal *inter alia* with
conduct of the homes and the provision of facilities and
services but do not for example specify what is 'adequate'
staffing in order to secure the well-being of residents. The
Code of Practice, *Home Life*, which the Secretary of State
has asked local authorities to treat in the same light as
general guidance he is empowered to give, is more specific
but not, of course, mandatory.

2.11   **Disabled Persons (Service, Consultation and Representation)
Act 1986.**
Entitles disabled people to a written assessment of their need
for services and to have representatives present at the time
the assessments are made.

Chapter Two

Recommendations

1 DEFINITION OF VULNERABILITY

1.1 Elderly people who are vulnerable could be defined as being in need of some support, help and/or advice in order to prevent or postpone 'personal or social deterioration or breakdown'.[1] Without this , their level of dependency on others or their ability to manage their lives as they wish, might deteriorate to the point of necessitating their removal to institutional care, which is not their preferred option and might otherwise be prevented or postponed.

1.2 Although in practice all the legislation in Section Five, Chapter One contains some inherent shortcomings, it does provide a framework upon which a more effective system could be built.

2 A GENERAL POWER TO PROMOTE THE WELFARE OF OLD PEOPLE

2.1 The Health Services and Public Health Act (1968), Section 45[2] already empowers a local authority to promote the welfare of old people, albeit only with the approval of the Minister of Health and to such an extent as he may direct. However this Section is broad enough to form the basis of more comprehensive legislation, particularly as, since the DHSS circular 19/71, considerable experience has been gained over a number of years. This could, therefore, now be extended to become a general power, which would enable

---

[1]See Section Five, Chapter One, para 2.5, which refers to DHSS circular 19/71
[2]*Idem*

local authorities to formulate a comprehensive policy for the promotion of the welfare of elderly people in their area. It could theoretically also extend to the payment of cash grants if necessary.[3]

2.2   This leads to the first recommendation: that consideration be given to introducing a general power to promote the welfare of old people. This could be based on Chapter One, Section Five, paragraph 2.5 which refers to the Health Services and Public Health Act (1968).

2.3   This power could include giving 'advice, guidance and assistance' (as in Section 1 of the Child Care Act, 1980) and bring together the various provisions governing local authorities' powers under a general welfare section providing a framework for action, together with a circular of guidance or code of practice. This would only be a *power* to make resources available. There would be no unreasonable intrusion. It would, however, be an advantage if the authority could estimate the numbers of vulnerable elderly people in the area. Thus the authority would be more aware of potential calls on its resources, as well as more alerted to future needs and better able to plan accordingly, which would be a valuable development. Existing provisions (see Section Five, Chapter One), sometimes do refer specifically to elderly people, but more often they will be covered only insofar as they fall under some other category.

2.4   Under this general power the local authority could, for example, appoint an independent person to be a visitor to a vulnerable elderly person.[4] This would be particularly relevant for elderly people in hospitals or residential accommodation with little or no contact with their family or friends.

3 A NEW DUTY

3.1   The proposal for a general power, however, would not in itself ensure to *individual* vulnerable elderly people and their

---

[3] Cf. Child Care Act (1980), Section 1 and Social Work Scotland Act (1968), Section 12
[4] A model for this might be drawn from Section 11 of the Child Care Act 1980

carers the right to have their own particular needs assessed and considered. Therefore, in addition to any general provision, serious consideration should be given to the introduction of a new duty to be placed on the local authority, namely, a duty to consider the case of a vulnerable individual elderly person.

3.2 At present a local authority has no specific duty to investigate complaints, to respond to requests for help or support from individual elderly people or their carers nor to conduct multidisciplinary assessments. In theory a combination of good practice and adequate resources would ensure that vulnerable elderly people have their needs and those of their carers met.[5] However in the real world there is intense competition for very limited resources and some form of legislation is needed, designed to meet the needs of this vulnerable group of people and giving them and their carers access to consideration and an assessment of their needs for support and care. The goal would be to ensure that suitably qualified people would be obliged to listen and to duly consider what, if anything, needed to be done. This would probably involve a multidisciplinary case conference in which the vulnerable elderly person's wishes would always be represented either in person or by a representative. It could then use its general power and notify the old person and the carer and take appropriate action.

3.3 This duty on a local authority would be to consider and assess the needs of a vulnerable elderly person and/or the carer of that person at the request of that elderly person, or the carer, or another person who was shown to have a proper interest. Once the local authority had considered the request and deemed it not to be frivolous, it could then use its powers to take appropriate action and to notify the old person and the carer accordingly.

3.4 It is significant that the initiators of the Disabled Persons (Service, Consultation and Representation) Act 1986

---

[5] Section 2(1) Children and Young Persons Act (1969) lays a duty on the local authority to cause enquiries to be made if they receive information suggesting that there are grounds for bringing care proceedings

acknowledged the need for this type of approach. This will strengthen the rights of disabled people in giving them entitlement to a written assessment from social workers of the need for services and the right to have a representative present at all health and soical work assessments, examinations and meetings discussing their case.

3.5 In carrying out its duty to consider, the local authority would always:

1 consider and take into account the wishes expressed by the elderly person and assess that person's needs;

2 assess the need of the carer for support and help in the tasks being carried out on behalf of the vulnerable elderly person and in providing care;

3 review the needs of the elderly person and/or the carer at intervals of not more than 12 months, until or unless the review considers this to be unnecessary;

4 consider whether it would be appropriate to appoint an independent person to be a 'visitor' as referred to in 2.4 above.

3.6 It is recognized that some requests from old people or carers would be for practical support or services which would not necessitate full multidisciplinary assessment.

3.7 It is also acknowledged that services cannot always be provided on demand and that resources are limited, but a duty on the local authority to consider the needs and circumstances of such people could ensure that some response to expressed need was forthcoming.

4 PROCEDURE: STAGE I

4.1 Given that the vulnerable elderly person satisfied the criteria for the initial consultative process, a plan of action, taking account of available resources, could be prepared.

4.2 This process would permit the continued operation of present good practice within the legal framework of a duty imposed on the local authority to consider what action, if any, was required. This process might frequently necessitate a degree of cooperation with other agencies, as is now the case.

5 PROCEDURE: STAGE II – ASSESSMENT

5.1 In cases where a more thorough investigation of circumstances and needs was required to meet a request for help or support, the local authority, to carry out its duty, would need to consult with those people who were interested in and knew about the situation of the old person. This group would include the old person and the primary carer. If it was considered inappropriate to include any of those people, a record would be made giving the reason for their exclusion. This procedure might necessitate a full multidisciplinary assessment.

5.2 A duty to consider would be of help in cases of suspected old age abuse as it would empower the local authority and other agencies to consider each case and would provide the mechanism for limited powers of intervention to assess the situation while respecting an individual's right to refuse help. If in the end a person did refuse help and was neither mentally incompetent nor under threat or duress, no action would be taken. Equally important, however, such a duty would enable potential 'abusers', who might be family members, to seek help when they could no longer cope and through it to prevent a tragedy.

5.3 After due consideration of all relevant circumstances, the decision might be:

1 that no further action should be taken;
2 that a plan of care should be prepared and steps taken to implement it;
3 that all steps the local authority was empowered to take had already been taken but that further intervention was still required.

6 PROCEDURE: STAGE III – NOTIFICATION

6.1 In any event and whichever course of action was taken, written reasons for the decision would need to be given. The elderly person, the carer and any other party having a proper interest would be informed of the decision and of the reasons for making it. If a plan of care was proposed, the consent of the elderly person would have to be sought. The proposed support services might not be under the direct control of the local authority. Drawing up the plan of care would be, therefore, the responsibility of the local authority, but this would inevitably require support from other bodies amongst whom might be included the GP, the Family Practitioner Committee, the health authority and the DHSS. Help might be available from many sources, including other statutory and voluntary bodies, in implementing the plan of action.

6.2 The old person, the carer and other interested parties might be dissatisfied with the decision. Any interested party would be able to request the director of social services to reconsider the decision and if necessary to hold an assessment or a further assessment, possibly specifying other parties that should be consulted.

6.3 The director of social services would have to provide a decision in writing and within a specified time. If the elderly person did not agree with the decision or consent to the proposed plan, s/he would have the right to refuse it.

7 PROCEDURE: STAGE IV – INTERVENTION ORDER

7.1 If the local authority *refused* to consider or, after consideration, failed to respond appropriately, the old person or someone acting on his or her behalf and with his or her consent, could apply to the court as an avenue of appeal against the decision of the local authority. Therefore, the purpose of an Intervention Order would be to provide a means of appealing against the action or failure to act by the local authority in carrying out its duty to consider the case of a vulnerable old person[6] and also in order to satisfy vulnerable old people and their carers, who would be able to achieve a recognized status through an Intervention Order, as they could be joined as parties, that the local authority's actions were in the best interests of that person and in the light of available resources.

---

[6] As is the case under Section 3 of the Children and Young Persons Act (1963)

7.2   On the other hand, should the local authority consider that the plan it had proposed was necessary and in the best interests of the old person, who refused it, the local authority would also have the right to take the matter to the court which would be empowered to review the decisions that had been taken. In the last resort the local authority could apply to the court for an Intervention Order, but only if it had demonstrably tried all other reasonable solutions to a serious problem.

7.3   On receipt of the application, which would have to provide evidence that the above stages had been followed and exhausted, the court would serve notice on all interested parties and a preliminary hearing would be held before a registrar within a specified time limit. At the preliminary hearing the registrar would:

1 need to be satisfied that the local authority had duly considered the matter and, in the case of an application by a party other than the local authority, that the director of social services of the local authority had been requested to reconsider the case and had done so;

2 ensure adequate representation of the person in respect of whom the application was made and order that appropriate arrangements were made for this;

3 when appropriate, request the preparation of reports from the local authority, a medical practitioner, a court welfare officer or specialist social worker, and any other person or body that the court might direct;

4 give directions generally including the joinder of certain other interested persons as parties, with the consent of the old person;

5 consider whether proceedings under the Mental Health Act were more appropriate.

6 if the old person refused to cooperate in the preparation of such a report, note this fact as a report in itself.

7.4   All parties eligible for legal aid would be able to apply for it.

7.5   In considering the application the judge would need to consider the interests of the vulnerable old person as paramount and due consideration would need to be given to his or her wishes. Steps would be taken to obtain evidence as to the wishes of the old person as the court thought fit.

7.6 The court would have to be satisfied that the local authority had taken all proper action and complied with the minimum precautions outlined in the procedure.

7.7 On hearing an application for an Intervention Order and after having heard oral evidence the court could make any of the following orders:

1 that the arrangements for the care of the old person, which existed immediately prior to the application, had been and were still satisfactory and no order was necessary.

2 that the local authority, together if necessary with the appropriate health authority and such other bodies and persons as the court thought fit, be recommended to take such steps as the court deemed necessary, with the old person's consent, to secure the well-being and necessary care and attention of that person.

3 that reports from specified persons or agencies be made to the court or to the local authority at intervals of not more than six months.

4 on finding that an old person was unable to attend to his or her affairs satisfactorily, that a representative of the old person be appointed. This representative could be a relative, carer, social worker or voluntary worker and would seek to express the best interests of the old person and would have the right to be consulted before any decisions were implemented.

5 that the matter be referred to the Court of Protection.

7.8 Any party would have the right to apply to the court, on notice to all other parties, for an order for the variation or discharge of any order already made by the court.
Intervention Order hearings would need to be *in camera*.

8 EMERGENCY POWERS

8.1 In exceptional circumstances of emergency when immediate action was needed to relieve a situation of immediate grave risk, direct application to the court could be possible without preliminary intervention by the local authority.

8.2 Upon application of any party who could satisfy the court of having a proper interest in the welfare of the old person a judge could make an Emergency Intervention Order for a maximum period of seven days renewable for a further seven days once only.

8.3 An Emergency Intervention Order could direct

1 that specific help be brought to the old person where s/he resides, subject to the availability of such help;
2 that the old person be removed to a place of safety;
3 that named individuals be restrained from assaulting, molesting or otherwise interfering with the old person or be excluded from the old person's home.

8.4 The application could only be made to a judge who would have to consider the same points referred to in 7.3 above. In addition the judge would have to be satisfied that unless an Emergency Intervention Order were granted there would be an immediate serious risk to the life, or safety of the old person.

8.5 Such application might be made in the first instance, and in exceptional circumstances only, *ex parte,* but not an application for renewal.

8.6 At the expiry of the order, the judge would hold a preliminary hearing at which he would consider all the matters which a registrar would do in the course of an Intervention Order.

8.7 If a general power to promote the welfare of elderly people were introduced together with a duty to consider their individual needs and those of their carers, there could still be an argument that some specific direction might be required as to the exercise of that power, but this is by no means certain and could prove to be unnecessary.

8.8 Should family courts be introduced in this country it would seem appropriate that procedures relating to vulnerable elderly people should fall within their jurisdiction.

9 SUMMARY

9.1 To summarize, the proposals laid out in this chapter for further discussion and detailed consideration are as follows:

9.2 **1** that a general power be introduced enabling local authorities:
a) to promote the welfare of elderly people and
b) advise, guide and assist old people and to make available resources as necessary
2 that a specific duty on local authorities be introduced to consider the case of individual vulnerable old people
3 that an Intervention Order be introduced to enable individual old people and/or their carers to oppose or to appeal against a decision of the local authority and to enable a local authority to oppose or appeal against the decision of an individual
4 that the above legislation be backed up by limited Emergency Powers.

9.3 It is believed that the above procedure, i.e. the duty to consider and the means of obtaining an Intervention Order, and an Emergency Intervention Order in extreme circumstances, would be helpful in cases of suspicion of a dangerous level of self-neglect, abuse by others or anxiety over the deteriorating condition of health of an old person. It would enable the local authority to assess what, in its view, was needed to avoid a potential tragedy. If the old person refused help, services or other support measures, and efforts to provide all appropriate and feasible domiciliary help of this type had been made and were recorded, the local authority would demonstrably have tried all other reasonable alternatives before seeking to 'intervene'. The emergency powers in this legislation would be very firmly limited and by emphasizing the primary duty of the court to consider the interests of the old person, that person, as an adult, would have the right to refuse any intervention and to make that known to the court. In such circumstances, the local authority would also itself be better protected and less open to criticism if, after refusing help, an old person became seriously ill, injured him or herself or died.

9.4 By building in the safeguards of the Intervention Order, the emergency powers described above would avoid the worst aspects of Section 47 of the National Assistance Act while retaining a means of protecting people in situations of grave risk or danger. The Intervention Order has built-in representation and acknowledges the role and experience of the principal carer and others with an intimate knowledge of a particular vulnerable old person's life style and wishes. Full consultation would be ensured together with regular reviews of the old person's situation, guided by the principle that prime consideration be given to the interests and welfare of the old person. As with a Place of Safety Order, drastic action could only be taken in emergency situations and reviewed after a very short period by the court.

9.5   **If these proposals were to be accepted, and, through them elderly people better supported in the community at an early stage, the need for expensive long-term residential and/or hospital care for some vulnerable old people, who wish to stay in their own homes, would be postponed, if not averted altogether, and their quality of life significantly improved.**

Further Reading

Law and Old People in Australia, National Research Institute for Gerontology and Geriatric Medicine, Occasional Paper No 5, June 1983: contains extensive bibliography (pp 16–68) and lists legislation affecting old people, both Commonwealth and State, in Australia.

The Role of the Elderly in the Family in the Context of the Society of the 1980s, Council of Europe, 1983.

APPENDICES

Addresses

Action for the Victims of
Medical Accidents
24 Southwark Street
London SE1 1TY

Advocacy Alliance
2nd Floor
115 Golden Lane
London EC1Y 0TS

Age Concern England
Bernard Sunley House
60 Pitcairn Road
Mitcham
Surrey CR4 3LL

Age Concern
Northern Ireland
6 Lower Crescent
Belfast
Northern Ireland
BT7 1NR

Age Concern Scotland
33 Castle Street
Edinburgh EH2 4DN

Age Concern Wales
1 Park Grove
Cardiff CF1 1YF

British Association for Service
to the Elderly
119 Hassell Street
Newcastle-under-Lyme
Staffordshire ST5 1AX

British Association of Social
Workers (BASW)
16 Kent Street
Birmingham B5 6RD

British Geriatric Society
1 St Andrew's Place
London NW1 4LB

British Paediatric Association
5 St Andrew's Place
London NW1 4LB

Centre for Policy on Ageing
25-31 Ironmonger Row
London EC1V 3QP

Centre for Social Studies in
Ageing (CESSA)
Polytechnic of North
London
Ladbroke House,
Highbury Grove
London N5 2AD

Court of Protection
Staffordshire House
25 Store Street
London WC1E 7BF

Disability Alliance Educational
and Research Association
25 Denmark Street
London WC2H 8NS

National Association for Mental
Health (MIND)
22 Harley Street
London W1N 2ED

Bibliography

1 OFFICIAL REPORTS

Residential Care for the Elderly in London, HMSO 1978

Olive Stevenson and Phyllida Parsloe, *Social Services Teams: the Practitioner's View,* DHSS, 1978

Elder Abuse: The Hidden Problem, prepared for the House Select Committee on Aging, 96 Cons: 1st Session (Comm Print 1979)

General Household Survey, HMSO, 1980

Growing Older, Cmnd 8173, HMSO 1981

Population Projections 1979–2019, Office of Population Censuses and Surveys, HMSO, 1981

The Incapacitated Principal, Law Commission No 122, Cmnd 8977, HMSO, 1983

Mental Health Act 1983, HMSO 1983

Biennial Report of the Mental Health Act Commission, 1985 (Section 8.15) Disabled Persons (Services Consultation and Representation) Bill 1985

Inspection of Local Authority Care for Elderly Mentally Disordered Patients, Social Services Inspectorate of the Department of Health and Social Security, DHSS, 1985

Code of Practice (Draft), Mental Health Act (1983), DHSS, 1985

Protecting Patients – Guidelines for Handling Staff Complaints about Patients' Care, National Association of Health Authorities in England and Wales, 1985

Consent to Treatment, HMSO, 1986

Social Trends, HMSO, 1986

2 BOOKS

Age Concern Wants Action on Dementia, Age Concern Scotland, 1986

Nicholas Bosanquet, *A Future for Old Age,* Temple Smith/New Society, 1978

Paul Brearley, Jim Black, Penny Gutridge, Gwyneth Roberts and Elizabeth Tarran, *Leaving Residential Care,* Tavistock, 1982

David Carson, *Mental Handicap and the Law: an Overview — Protection versus Restriction of the Vulnerable,* Faculty of Law, University of Southampton, 1985

Christopher Cloke, *Old Age Abuse in the Domestic Setting — a Review,* Age Concern England, 1983

Dementia in Scotland — Priorities for Care, Strategies for Change, Scottish Action on Dementia, 1986

Disability Rights Handbook, published annually by the Disability Alliance Educational and Research Association

The Elderly Consumer, National Consumer Council, 1982

Caroline Faulder, *Whose Body Is It?* Virago, 1985

M L M Gilhooly, S H Zarit, and J E Birren (eds) *The Dementias: Policy and Management,* Prentice Hall, New Jersey

Larry Gostin, *The Court of Protection: A Legal and Policy Analysis of the Guardianship of the Estate,* MIND, 1983

Richard Grimes, *Law and the Elderly,* Croom Helm, 1986

Handbook of Living Will Laws, 1981–1984, Society for the Right to Die (US), 1984

John Harris, *The Value of Life,* Routledge & Kegan Paul, 1985

Home Life: A Code of Practice for Residential Care, Report of a Working Party sponsored by the Department of Health and Social Security and convened by the Centre for Policy on Ageing under the Chairmanship of Kina, Lady Avebury. Centre for Policy on Ageing, 1984

Marshall B Kapp, Harvey E Pies, Jr., A. Edward Doudera (eds) *Legal and Ethical Aspects of Health Care for the Elderly.* American Society of Law and Medicine, Health Administration Press, Ann Arbor, Michigan, 1985

Leonie Kellaher, Sheila Peace, Dianne Willcocks, *Living in Homes: A Consumer View of Old People's Homes,* BASE/CESSA, 1985

William Laing, *Private Health Care,* Office of Health Economics, 1985

Neil Leighton, Richard Stalley and David Watson, *Rights and Responsibilities,* Heinemann/Community Care, 1982

Michael Lockwood (ed), *Moral Dilemmas in Modern Medicine,* Oxford University Press, 1986

Nancy L Mace, Peter V Rabins et al, *The 36-Hour Day,* Hodder and Stoughton/Age Concern England, 1985

Jill Manthorpe, *Elderly People: Rights and Opportunities,* Longman, 1986

Mary Marshall, *Social Work with Old People, Macmillan, 1983*

L McDerment and S Greengross, (eds), *Social Care for Elderly People: An International Perspective,* Social Care Association, 1986

Alison Norman, *Rights and Risk,* Centre for Policy on Ageing, 1980

Alison Norman, *Mental Illness in Old Age: Meeting the Challenge,* Centre for Policy on Ageing, 1984

Melanie Phillips and John Dawson, *Doctors' Dilemmas,* Harvester Press, 1985

J Rachels, *The End of Life: Euthanasia and Morality,* Oxford University Press, 1986

P Riga, *Right to Die or Right to Live? Legal Aspects of Death and Dying,* Tarrytown, NY, Associated Faculty Press, 1981

The Role of the Elderly in the Family in the Context of the Society of the 1980s, Council of Europe, 1983

N St John-Stevas, *Life, Death and the Law: A Study of the Relationship Between Law and Christian Morals in the English and American Legal Systems,* Littleton, Colo: Rothman, 1981

Anthea Tinker, The Elderly in Modern Society, Longman, 1984 (Second edition)

Alan Walker, *The Care Gap: How Can Local Authorities Meet the Needs of the Elderly?* Local Government Information Unit, 1985

Tim Weaver, Dianne Willcocks, and Leonie Kellaher, *The Pursuit of Profit and Care: Patterns and Processes in Private Residential Homes for Old People,* CESSA, 1985

Monica Wilson, *The College of Health Guide to Homes for Elderly People,* College of Health, 1984

Rosalie Wolf, Michael Godkin and Karl Pillemer, *Elder Abuse and Neglect: Final Report from the Three Model Projects,* University of Massachusetts, 1984

Working with Abused Elders: Assessment, Advocacy and Intervention, University Center on Aging, University of Massachusetts, 1984

Legislation in Northern Ireland

Section Two ▪ *Chapter Two*
COMPULSORY REMOVAL FROM HOME:
>
> The equivalent power is found in Art. 37 and Schedule 6 of the Health and Personal Social Services (NI) Order 1972

Section Two ▪ *Chapter Three*
ADMISSION TO CARE:
>
> The relevant legislation is the Health & Personal Social Services (NI) Order 1972 and Health & Personal Social Services (Registration of Homes) Regulations 1973; the Nursing Homes and Nursing Agencies Act (NI) 1971 and Nursing Homes (Registration, Conduct and Records) Regulations (NI) 1975.

Section Two ▪ *Chapter Four*
CONSENT TO TREATMENT:
>
> The general common law principles apply equally in Northern Ireland.
> The Mental Health Act (NI) 1961 is the relevant legislation, but will probably be replaced in 1986.

Section Three ▪ *Chapter One*
THE COURT OF PROTECTION:
>
> The equivalent to the Court of Protection is the Office of Care and Protection. See Mental Health Act (NI) 1961 as amended by Schedule 3 and Schedule 5 of the Judicature (NI) Act 1978; the Draft Mental Health (NI) Order 1986 especially Part II (Guardianship) and Part VIII (the Management of Property and Affairs of Patients).

Section Four ▪ *Chapter Four*
POWERS OF ATTORNEY:
>
> The Enduring Powers of Attorney Act 1985 does not substantially apply to Northern Ireland. See Powers of Attorney Act (NI) 1971.